P9-CAA-479

The Best of Regional Thai Cuisine

Hippocrene is NUMBER ONE
in International Cookbooks

Africa and Oceania
Best of Regional African Cooking
Egyptian Cooking
Good Food from Australia
Traditional South African Cookery
Taste of Eritrea

Asia and Near East
The Best of Taiwanese Cuisine
Imperial Mongolian Cooking
The Joy of Chinese Cooking
The Best of Regional Thai Cuisine
Japanese Home Cooking
Healthy South Indian Cooking
The Indian Spice Kitchen
Best of Goan Cooking
Best of Kashmiri Cooking
Afghan Food and Cookery
The Art of Persian Cooking
The Art of Turkish Cooking
The Art of Uzbek Cooking

Mediterranean
Best of Greek Cuisine
Taste of Malta
A Spanish Family Cookbook
Tastes of North Africa

Western Europe
Art of Dutch Cooking
Best of Austrian Cuisine
A Belgian Cookbook
Cooking in the French Fashion
    (bilingual)
Celtic Cookbook
Cuisines of Portuguese Encounters
English Royal Cookbook
The Swiss Cookbook
Traditional Recipes from Old England
The Art of Irish Cooking
Feasting Galore Irish-Style
Traditional Food from Scotland
Traditional Food from Wales
The Scottish-Irish Pub and Hearth
    Cookbook
A Treasury of Italian Cuisine (bilingual)

Scandinavia
Best of Scandinavian Cooking
The Best of Finnish Cooking
The Best of Smorgasbord Cooking
Good Food from Sweden
Tastes & Tales of Norway
Icelandic Food & Cookery

Central Europe
All Along the Rhine
All Along the Danube
Best of Albanian Cooking
Best of Croatian Cooking
Bavarian Cooking
Traditional Bulgarian Cooking
The Best of Czech Cooking
The Best of Slovak Cooking
The Art of Hungarian Cooking
Hungarian Cookbook
Art of Lithuanian Cooking
Polish Heritage Cookery
The Best of Polish Cooking
Old Warsaw Cookbook
Old Polish Traditions
Treasury of Polish Cuisine (bilingual)
Poland's Gourmet Cuisine
The Polish Country Kitchen Cookbook
Taste of Romania
Taste of Latvia

Eastern Europe
The Best of Russian Cooking
Traditional Russian Cuisine (bilingual)
The Best of Ukrainian Cuisine

Americas
A Taste of Quebec
Argentina Cooks
Cooking the Caribbean Way
Mayan Cooking
The Honey Cookbook
The Art of Brazilian Cookery
The Art of South American Cookery
Old Havana Cookbook (bilingual)

The Best of Regional Thai Cuisine

by
Chat Mingkwan

HIPPOCRENE BOOKS
NEW YORK

Drawings by Pia Mingkwan.
Photographs by Chat Mingkwan.

Copyright © 2002 Chat Mingkwan.
All rights reserved.

Book and jacket design by Acme Klong Design, Inc.

For information, address:
HIPPOCRENE BOOKS, INC.
171 Madison Avenue
New York, NY 10016

ISBN 0-7818-0880-4

Cataloging-in-Publication data available from the Library of Congress.

Printed in the United States of America.

CONTENTS

*To my daughter, PIA, whose smiles bring me back from
the depths of discouragement.*

Without smiles, what would the human race be?

*A portion of the proceeds from this book will be donated
to projects that promote the preservation of endangered wildlife.
With your help, they'll keep on roaming.*

A Mythical Creature

Thai food is represented fittingly by a creature in Thai mythology. This creature has the head of an elephant, the body of a lion, and wings sprouting from all four legs. It possesses the best qualities in each of these animals: the strength of an elephant, the power of a lion, and the ability to fly.

Thai people have always had ability to replicate, adapt, and modify native flavors to suit Thai tastes. Accordingly, Thai food is a hybrid, influenced by the many cuisines the Thai people have tasted over time, and contains the best qualities of each; these qualities have been incorporated to produce classical Thai dishes.

The Chinese brought gifts of noodles and the techniques of wok cooking to the Thais; Thais in turn modified a Chinese stir-fried dish into the classical and popular *Pad Thai*. The Indians offered colorful, fragrant curries; combined with Thai herbs and seasonings, these curries incorporated the best from the two countries: yellow, green, and red curries. Cambodia, Indonesia, Laos, Malaysia, Myanmar (Burma), and Vietnam border Thailand, each having established a history of both sweet and bitter relationships. Each has also contributed greatly to make Thai food as complex, complete, and agreeable as it is today.

ACKNOWLEDGEMENTS

Often, a misconception comes first, then fear. Many exotic taste-seekers enjoy fully flavored and aromatic Thai food. But most hesitate to take on Thai cooking. Recipes appear complicated and the names are foreign. The food is expected to always be hot and spicy. The ingredients are unfamiliar and hard to find. In addition to these misconceptions, fear steps in—fear of the unknown, uncertainty, failure, and embarrassment. I now offer you a solution to overcome this fear and become a Thai food connoisseur.

Thai cuisine, like any other, has unique characteristics. Ever since childhood, I've been learning and perfecting my recipes so they will be easy for you to follow and master. I've enough confidence to share my recipes with those who are already drawn to Thai food, and also enough courage to convince those who misunderstand Thai cooking to give it another try.

Cooking Thai food is easier than most people think. To understand Thai food is to understand its ingredients and simple techniques. Then, eating it often will help you recognize its tastes and flavors. In no time, as many of my students will attest, you can become a proficient Thai cook.

In the process of gathering and perfecting recipes, my students' tongues were the testing ground. They've been through the trials of executing and tasting recipes; my beginning classes have given me insight into the Thai cook's first experience, and my intermediate and advanced students show how they take the ingredients and techniques to the next level. I have used this valuable information to modify and perfect each recipe to fit the Western kitchen and suit food enthusiasts of all levels.

During several trips back to Thailand, my brothers Chai and Chay and their families and friends have indulged me with their best offerings. They've introduced me to new trends and popular local restaurants. I've tasted the best Thai food and pestered many chefs to get their recipes and learn their techniques, and I have even tried to pry their secrets out of them. My sister Tip and her husband Daeng, who live in a Thai community in the United States, have also greatly contributed to the authenticity of these recipes. Most of all, I extend my gratitude to friends and supporters who truly believe in my ability and encourage me to share my knowledge and skills, and also to nonbelievers who keep me going.

Perseverance was a key to finishing this book, as English is my second language and as perfecting recipes has taken innumerable trials. I wish to thank my gentle and kind friends and associates for guiding me through my language difficulties and repeatedly tasting my food samples. My daughter Pia brings me back from the depths of discouragement every times she smiles at me.

With a steady pace, you need less than half of my efforts and perseverance to understand Thai food. There are only few basic ingredients essential to Thai cooking, and nowadays, they occupy the ethnic food section in most supermarkets.

I hope that my recipes, with these simple instructions, will lead you to an epicurean experience and to a better understanding of Thai culinary art, and, most important, to making the cooking of Thai food into a fun and exciting experience to share with your families and friends.

Sawasdee,

Chat Mingkwan

INTRODUCTION

Since my early childhood, I remember Thailand as "The Land of the Smile," where Thais always smile and are hospitable beyond bounds. I can still cite a poem that captured the Thai attitude of hospitality very well.

ประเพณีไทยแท้แต่โบราณ	*The tradition of Thais has lasted long, for centuries*
ใครมาถึงเรือนชานต้องต้อนรับ	*where guests are welcomed with unconditional hospitality.*
ทั้งเลิศดีตามมีและตามเกิด	*We give the best of what we have to offer,*
ให้เพลิดเพลินกายากว่าจะกลับ	*ensure an utmost pleasant stay till the guests' departure.*

And how could hospitality be easier than providing the best food to our guests?

In Thailand, I believe food is not only essential for existing, but also for being Thai. Often, the Thais greet each other with the question: *"Khin Khao Roue Yung?"* (Have you eaten yet?). If you visit a Thai friend or relative, he or she or the whole family will welcome you with all kinds of food and drink. No matter how hard you insist on saying no or explaining that you have just eaten, offerings still keep coming. To say no to food is impolite. So you eat and taste and praise the food as if it were divine. At the same time, you blame the host for making you so full and fat because of nonstop eating. Thais often tease each other with nonsense and silly gestures as terms of endearment. I often hear the word *ooun*, which means fat, and is a popular nickname. Calling someone "fat" is light-hearted fun and acceptable in Thai culture, since the fat represents a well-to-do and leisurely lifestyle.

Thai people use the word *sanuk* or "fun" to describe degree of pleasure in all activities. Eating is considered *sanuk*, and it should be fun because Thais, when an opportunity arises, always treat their meal as an indulgence. The Buddhist teaching that life is suffering, impermanence, and constant change also contributes to the Thai attitude of *sanuk* as Thais often take one day at a time. Most leisure activities will include eating in order to double the fun. The Thais eat around the clock. There are snacks, heavy meals, and sweets, each designated for a certain time of the day. For example, *Pla Tong Goo*, deep-fried savory dough, is a breakfast treat and the pastry maker only produces it at the crack of dawn. *Kanom Jeen*, a heavy curry dish, is for lunch or dinner. But who enforces all these rules? Some of us in the United States have found that a leftover cold pizza is great for breakfast; likewise, most Thai people find a meal edible at any time.

Easy access to food also influences the way the Thais eat. Local merchants usually set up food stands and offer a variety on sidewalks at major intersections where people gravitate. For a family that doesn't have much time to prepare dinner, this is a great open market for conveniently choosing a daily special at a very reasonable price. Food is fresh and ready to be packed and taken home. I have found some of the best Thai dishes at the sidewalk food stands. The taste is undeniably delicious since the merchants rely on a reputation built from word of mouth and repeated customers, not to mention threat of competitors.

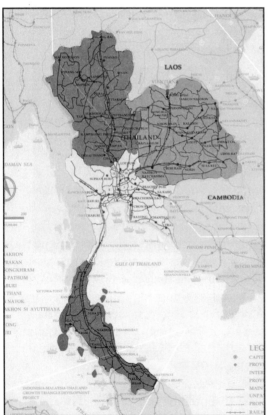

Geographically, Thailand is divided into four distinct regions: North, Northeast, Central, and South. Each has its own unique character, climate, language, personality and, of course, cuisine. This book devotes one chapter to each region. Each chapter describes the character and cuisine, and includes popular regional recipes for snacks, appetizers, salads, soups, curries, and main courses. The last chapter combines desserts and beverages from all the regions. With precise standard measurements in each recipe, you can follow the simple instructions and prepare a delicious meal. All recipes have been tested and tasted several times by both beginning and advanced students in my cooking classes until they reached satisfying results.

The Best of Regional Thai Cuisine

EATING THAI-THAI

The first Thai in Thai-Thai means freedom, as in the spirit of Thai people, whose independence has been maintained over the centuries against formidable western powers of colonization. The second Thai means Thai food and style. Eating anything, anytime, and anywhere seems to best capture the meaning of eating Thai-Thai.

Though each region has distinct differences in cuisine, one uniting factor is the way Thais eat. A number of Thais eat together, usually with a group of family and friends from a tightly knit support system. To eat alone is considered bad luck. A number of dishes are prepared or ordered to be shared, the amount often being more than enough for everyone. A house cook always makes extra food for unexpected quests or for a second serving. So most of the home-cooked meal will usually be a combination of new and leftover dishes. Children in the family are told to eat the leftovers first. But adults always end up eating them or giving them to the pets, including pigs in some households. Some dishes, such as *Hung Lay* curry, taste better on the second day. Often, the leftover is transformed into a new dish. The most popular one of these is the stew-like *Jub Chay*, a combination of leftover meats and vegetables with new herbs and spices. The Thais hardly ever throw food away, especially rice. Thais believe in *Mae Pro Sob*, the god of rice who looks over the people's well being and the abundance of food. Wasting will displease her and her anger could result in a famine and starvation.

Adapting to Western nomenclature, Thai food can be categorized as appetizers, soups, salads, main courses, and desserts. But in reality, all dishes except the dessert are served at the same time and can be eaten in any order. Rice is an essential component in every meal and there is always plenty of it; either steamed white rice, glutinous sweet rice, or rice porridge, depending on the region and the meal. A Thai meal traditionally consists of several dishes with a combination of flavors: sweet, hot, sour, and salty. Two to three types of meat are used to provide variety in taste and texture. A typical combination consists of a sharp-flavored salad and plenty of fresh vegetables; a soup, including curry dishes; a stir-fry of meat and vegetables; a meat dish such as deep-fried fish or fried chicken; and a basic sauce or chili dip, *namprik*, with a side dish of vegetables. The dessert is made with a sweet base of coconut or a variety of seasonal fruits.

Occasionally, for convenience and to save time, a one-dish meal, such as a noodle soup, fried rice, or curry and rice is quite popular. But there is always an accompaniment of vegetables, sauces, or condiments. *Prik Nam Som* (chilies in vinegar) is as important for the noodle soup as *Nam Pla Prik* (fresh chilies in fish sauce) is for the fried rice, and *Prik Poan* (crushed dried chilies) is for those needing extra heat.

Glossary of Ingredients

Thai food is characterized by the four tastes: sweet, sour, hot, and salty. The Thais frequently use palm sugar for sweet, lime and tamarind for sour, chilies for hot, and fish sauce for salty. Some of the ingredients are new to Western kitchens, though they are accessible through Asian markets in U.S. towns. Don't be put off by unfamiliar ingredients and techniques. Thai cooking is not a difficult and complicated process. In fact, by becoming familiar with the ingredients and their uses, lovers of Thai food can easily prepare any dish on a Thai menu. Only unfamiliar ingredients to the Western kitchen are mentioned in this chapter including where to find and how to use them.

HERBS and SPICES

What make Thai food unique are special herbs and spices. The ingredients and cooking methods from neighboring countries have greatly influenced Thai cuisine. Thais have adopted the noodles from the Chinese to create the classic dish *Pad Thai* (see recipes and article pages 151-157). Curries from India have filtered into Thai households and been modified for Thai taste. Surprisingly, from as far away as Central America, chilies have traveled on Spanish and Portuguese fleets to land on fertile Thai soil to become part of the signature spicy Thai dishes. These herbs and spices usually grow in tropical climates and find their way to the Western countries. Nowadays, fresh Thai herbs and spices can be produced in the United States, especially in the hot climates of Florida and Hawaii, and in California during the summer months. As the popularity of Thai and Southeast Asian cuisine grows, so does the market for these popular herbs and spices. Thai sweet basil, bird's-eye chilies, and fish sauce earn their shelf spaces commercially in the big-name grocery stores.

As weather permits, I cultivate my own Thai herb garden. Some of them do well in the ground and some are very content in pots. Most nurseries now carry exotic herbs in seed and starter plant form for both cooking and decorative purposes. Most of the herbs are perennial and do very well during hot months in the ground. The ones in pots are conveniently moved indoors during severe weather and are able to last for two to three years. Though most of the Thai herbs and spices can be cultivated locally, some have to be imported in various forms: fresh, dried, powdered, frozen, and canned in brine. Some herbs and spices can easily find substitutions outside Thailand, but to maintain an authentic essence, the herbs and spices with an asterisk (★) can't be substituted.

BASIL: Three kinds of basil are used in Thai cooking. At a very young age, I first learned to cook by identifying their different flavors, appearances, and uses. If I was sent to the market, I often came back with all three kinds of basil to avoid mistakes. It may be hard to find the exact basil to use. Substitute among each other or use Italian basils.

Thai Sweet Basil, *Bai Horapha (Ocimum basilicum)*, has small flat green leaves with pointy tips and the stems and flowers are sometimes reddish purple. It imparts very intensive taste with an anise or licorice flavor. It's often used for flavoring garnishes over coconut curries and for leafy vegetable. Ordinary sweet basil makes a good substitute.

Lemon Basil, *Bai Mangluk (Ocimum carnum),* has light green leaves with slight speckle of hairs, green stems, and sometimes with white flowers. It has a nippy peppery and lemon flavor that goes well with soup and salad, especially with *Kanom Jeen*, curry noodle.

Holy Basil, *Bai Kaprow (Ocimum sanctum),* has distinctive violet-reddish hue on both leaves and stems. It imparts mint-like, zesty, and very spicy flavor—used for stir-fries such as *Pad Bai Kapao*, stir-fried meat with basil.

CARDAMOM:* *Luk Kravan (Elettaria cardamomum)* is indigenous to India and Sri Lanka. Cardamom has a eucalyptus-like lemony flavor. It is used a lot in Muslim-style curries of the South.

CHILI: Smaller means hotter. *Prik Khee Nu* is the smallest and hottest kind of chili, and the same name is often used to convey a message of small but powerful. For example, in Thai boxing, a small but capable boxer with odds and sizes against him is dubbed *Lek Prik Khee Nu*, which means he has much tenacity and a chance to win. For chilies, the smaller represents more heat.

Bird's-Eye Chilies, *Prik Khee Nu Suan (Capiscum minimum)* literally "mouse droppings," are the smallest with red or green color and the most pungent taste. They are used for chili sauces and dips, and added to curry pastes for spicy heat. Bird's-eye chilies are available in most Asian grocery stores under the label Thai chilies.

Prik Chee Fa *(Capsicum frutescens)*, come in red, yellow, or green and are the size of a forefinger. They look similar to a jalapeño with a pointy tip. They are a lot milder than the bird's-eye chilies and are used both fresh and dried. *Prik Haeng*, dried chilies, are for making the chili paste found in red, green, and yellow curry. If *Prik Chee Fa* are not available, use Mexican dried large chilies such as chile guajillo, California chilies, chili de arbol or Japones chilies.

dried chilies

Serrano *(Capiscum annum)* is a mid-green, smooth skin, pointed tip with rounded body chili, which is easily found in U.S. markets. It is as mild as the *Prik Chee Fa* and is multipurpose.

CHIVES: *Kui Chay (Allium schoenoprasum),* Chinese or garlic chives, have stronger aroma than European chives. They are available in flat long slender leaves and long stems topped with white flowers. They are used exclusively for stir-fry dishes such as *Pad Thai* and for garnish over noodle dishes. Green onion is a good substitute.

CILANTRO:* *Puk Chee (Coriandrum sativum)* or Chinese parsley is used indispensably and generously in Thai cooking. Each part of the plant from roots to leaves can be utilized for different purposes. The roots and seeds (also known as coriander seeds) are very pungent and important ingredients for making curry pastes and flavoring clear soup broth. The stems and leaves are used both for flavoring and leafy green garnish. Cilantro has light green, delicate leaves and stems with white or light pink flowers, which are all edible. In most U.S. supermarkets, the cilantro is sold without roots but stems can be substituted for roots in cooking. The coriander seeds are best used after being dry-roasted for stronger aroma. Like any other dry spices, seeds and ground coriander lose fragrance after 6 months.

CORIANDER:* see Cilantro.

CUMIN:* *Yee Ra (Cumimum cyminum)* or cumin seeds have a robust, exotic hearty aroma and flavor. One of the main ingredients in curry pastes. It is important to toast cumin seeds in a dry pan before grinding them.

GALANGAL:* *Kha (Alpinia officinarum)* or Siamese ginger is a perennial rhizome plant similar to ginger but has a larger and brighter colored root. The root tips are pink and have a strong medicinal taste and so can't be eaten directly like ginger. Galangal is used as a pungent ingredient in ground curry pastes and is used as a main herb for its unique and exotic aroma in popular sweet and sour *Tom Yum* and coconut galangal soup. Galangal can be found in fresh root, frozen, dry, and powder form in most Asian grocery stores. If using dried slices of galangal, soak them in warm water for at least 30 minutes or until you can bend the piece before putting them in a blender. Substitute the fresh galangal with half the amount of dry galangal in the recipe.

KAFFIR LIME:* *Magrood (Citrushysterix)* has a thick, dark, wrinkled skin. Its shinny rush green leaves, *Bai Magrood*, and rinds, *Pew Magrood*, are used for a strong citrus flavor in curry pastes, soups, and salads. They are available in Asian grocery stores in fresh, dry, and frozen form.

LEMONGRASS:* *Takrai (Cymbopogon citratus)* resembles a grass with a strong lemon aroma. To use the lemongrass, cut off the grassy top and root end. Peel and remove the large tough outer leaves of the stalk until you reach a light purple color. Chop it very fine to use in salads and grind into curry pastes or cut into 2-inch portions and bruise it to use in soup

broth. Lemongrass can be found fresh in most grocery stores because it has a very long shelf life. Dry and frozen forms are also available in most Asian stores.

LESSER GINGER:* *Krachai (Kaempferia pandurata)* is also rhizome plant, another relative of the ginger root but milder in flavor. *Krachai* comes in tubes, long, thin, and fingerlike with yellow meat and brown skin. It is a main ingredient for making a curry broth for *Kanom Jeen* noodles.

STAR ANISE:* *Poi Guk (Illicium verum)* is indigenous to China, uniquely shaped with an eight-pointed pod from a tree in the magnolia family. It has a warm, sweet, and strong anise flavor. Both whole and ground star anises are used in flavoring the broth for noodle soups and spice blends.

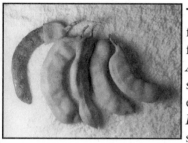

TAMARIND: *Makham (Tamarindus indica)* is a fruit pod of a very large tamarind tree with fine fernlike leaves. Fresh green tamarind, *Makham Awn*, can be used as in chili dips or pickled as a snack. The ripe brown pulp, *Makham Paek*, is extracted for tamarind liquid, *Nam Makham Paek*, and is used as a source of sour flavor with-  out the tartness of lime. The tamarind liquid is often used in soups and stir-fries. At the Asian grocery stores, it comes in a pulp block, powder, and ready-made in a can. To make tamarind liquid from a pulp, soak a 1-inch cube of tamarind with 1/2 cup of warm water. With your fingers, work the tamarind until disintegrated and the water turns brown and thickens. Strain the mixture through a sieve for the tamarind liquid.

TURMERIC:* *Kamin (Curcama domestica)* is another rhizome plant that is bright yellow-good for coloring and flavoring. The ground turmeric is used mainly in curry powders.

YANANG LEAVES: *Bai Yanang* are green leaves of a tropical tree. They are used mainly to counteract the bitter taste of other vegetables. Northeastern cuisine uses *Bai Yanang* in many dishes, such as the bamboo shoot salad in which *Bai Yanang* helps cut the bitter taste of the bamboo shoots. *Bai Yanang* liquid is made from boiling the leaves with water and extracting out the juice. *Bai Yanang* liquid in a can is available in Asian grocery stores.

VEGETABLES

Thai cooking sometimes calls for selected vegetables to maintain its authenticity and unique tastes. In Thailand, most of the vegetables are available year-round. In the United States, you can find the vegetables in well-stocked Asian stores and farmers' markets, especially in spring and summer months. Some hard-to-find varieties are imported fresh or available in preserved forms, such as canned, dried, and frozen. When available, fresh produce is worth tasting if you are willing to go to the trouble of preparing from scratch.

BABY CORN: *Khao Phot Awn* is young corn that has been harvested before maturity. It is very sweet and tender, and is used as a fresh vegetable to accompany chili dips, or is stir-fried with meats. Fresh baby corn is available in well-stocked Asian produce markets, but cooked and canned baby corn is widely available. There is no comparison in taste between fresh and canned baby corn.

BAMBOO SHOOTS: *Naw Mai (Phyllostachy bambusa* and *dendrocalamus)* is the young sprouts of the bamboo bush. It has a neutral taste with a crunchy texture, which absorbs flavors well in various Thai dishes, especially in curries. You can buy bamboo shoots fresh, cooked, or canned in some supermarkets. To prepare fresh bamboo shoots, trim the tips and remove tough outer shells; cut the bottom ends and boil with 2 to 3 changes of water until tender but still crunchy.

Pickled Bamboo Shoots: *Naw Mai Dong* are available for dishes that require a stronger flavor and sour taste. The pickled bamboo must be boiled with several changes of water to get rid of the pungent aroma.

BANANA FLOWER: *Hua Plee* is the male part at the tip of a banana flower where the female counterpart at the end develops into banana fruit. To prepare banana flower, remove the tough red outer petals and trim the stem back. Cut it in half and cook in boiling water for 15

to 20 minutes, then slice and add to soups or salads. The flower can be eaten raw as an accompaniment to a main dish. It needs to be soaked in water with lime or lemon juice or rubbed with a slice of lime to keep it from turning brown.

BANANA LEAF: *Bai Tong* is used primarily as a wrapper for steaming and grilling. It can also be used as a plate, bowl, or liner on serving platters, and is available both fresh and frozen. It must be washed and cut to shape before use.

CELERY: *Kheun Chai (Apium graveolens)* is known as Chinese celery, is smaller in size than western celery, and has a stronger flavor. It is served fresh in salads or cooked in clear broth and used mostly in seafood dishes to counteract the fishy flavor.

DAIKON: *Hua Chai Thao (Raphanus sativus)* is the root of a giant white radish, and has a long, cylindrical shape resembling a white carrot. Daikon is often used in Chinese-influenced Thai dishes.

EGGPLANT: *Ma-Kheua* comes in many varieties, ranging in size, shape, and color from a small marble to a baseball; from an egg shape to a sphere; and from white, yellow, and green to purple. Three varieties are frequently used:

Ma-Kheua Pro *(Salanum spp.)*, golf-ball size, light green with a crunchy texture; used as a vegetable in red or green curry and also served as a fresh vegetable with a chili dip.

Ma-Kheua Puang *(Solanum torvum)* grows in clusters with bright green color and is the size of small marbles.

Ma-Kheua Yao, a long green fruit with a denser texture than regular purple eggplant, often used in stir-fry dishes and salads.

KALE: *Phak Kana (Brassica oleracea)* or Chinese broccoli, *Gai Lan*, is a dark green, leathery leaf that grows on a thick stalk. Both the leaf and stalk can be eaten. Peel the tough skin off the stalk before use.

The Best of Regional Thai Cuisine

MORNING GLORY: see Swamp Cabbage.

MUSHROOM: *Het* is available in many varieties. The most common is the straw mushroom, *Het Fang*, which, unfortunately is only available in cans in the United States. *Het Hoi Nang Rom* is locally known as the oyster mushroom. *Het Hom*, shiitake mushroom, is available both fresh and dry. *Het Hu Nu*, mouse's-ear mushroom or wood ear mushroom, is also available both fresh and dry, and is appealing for its crunchy texture.

PANDAN LEAF: *Bai Toey (Pandanus odorus)* has a long, slender bright green leaf. Its extract provides a sweet fragrance and is used in making sweets. In Thailand, a bunch of pandan is often hung and used as an air freshener in a room or a car. In the United States, pandan is available in frozen and extract form.

PRESERVED TURNIP: *Hau Chai Po* or Chinese pickled radish is a salt-cured Chinese turnip or radish. It is a flavor enhancer, salty and sweet with a crunchy texture. Chop into small chunks before use. It is available in the dried goods section of all Asian markets.

SWAMP CABBAGE: *Phak Bung (Ipomoea aquatica)*, water spinach or aquatic morning glory, has roughly triangular-shaped leaves and hollow stems. The Thai variety has dark green leaves with red stalks while the Chinese type is lighter green and has thicker stalks. The tender tips are popular for flambé or stir-fry, or are eaten fresh as a side vegetable. Spinach is the closest substitute.

WATER CHESTNUT: *Haeo* gives a sweet flavor and crunchy texture to many dishes especially desserts. It is the tuber of a plant in the sedge family. Fresh water chestnuts are available at well-stocked Asian markets. Choose firm, unblemished ones. Peel off the black skin before use. Canned water chestnuts are available in all supermarkets.

WINGED BEAN: *Thua Phu* has a light green pod, which, in cross section, is rectangular with a fringe-like extension at each corner. Well-stocked Asian stores and farmers' markets offer the winged bean in spring and summer. Tender beans and peas are a good substitute.

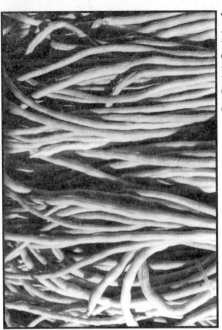

YARD-LONG BEAN: *Thua Fak Yao,* long bean or snake bean has green slender pods up to 12 inches long. It is excellent eaten raw or cooked in stir-fry dishes and is available in most supermarkets during spring and summer months.

FRUITS, NUTS, and SEEDS

Thailand produces many seasonal and year-round varieties of tropical fruit. A Thai fruit market is vibrant with colors and fragrances. In the United States, tropical fruits have gained popularity among consumers who seek exotic tastes. Mangoes, quince, lychees, and even durians are enjoyed by American palates. Some tropical fruits, seeds, and nuts can now be cultivated in the United States while most are usually imported fresh and preserved. When buying fruit, look for a nice bright color, ripe firm texture, and a sweet, pleasant aroma.

BANANA: *Kluai* is the most popular and abundant fruit in Thailand, where you can choose among thirty varieties. Three popular varieties readily found in the United States are *Kluai Nam Wa*, short pale, yellow oblong fruit (Mexican plantain can be substituted); *Kluai Hoam*, similar to regular bananas here; and *Kluai Kai* or baby banana, a small, almost round fruit with a distinctive sweet aroma.

CASHEW NUTS: *Med Mamoung Himmaphan* are grown abundantly in the South. It is the seed that develops outside the fruit of the mango. Cashew is sought after for its unique flavor and texture, and eaten alone as a snack or as an ingredient in many dishes. It is quite expensive even where it is grown.

COCONUT: *Ma-Prow (Cocos nucifera)* is the most versatile plant: its leaves and trunks are used in construction, its shells for fiber and in the garment industry, and its fruit for food and medicines. Coconut or palm sugar is extracted from the sap of the coconut flower, and palm wine or toddy is further refined by way of fermentation and distillation.

Ma-Prow Awn, young coconut, is popular for the clear, refreshing, flavorful drink often served with tender white coconut meat.

Ma-Prow Pow, smoked coconut, is young green coconut that has been smoked, a process that intensified flavors, giving a slightly smoky aroma.

Krati, coconut milk, is derived from processing the grated white meat of the ripe brown coconut, not to be confused with the clear coconut water. The process involves steeping the fresh-grated coconut meat in boiling water, and letting it stand for 5 to 10 minutes before pressing and straining out the thick white liquid. The first press is usually set aside for a rich coconut cream, *Hua Krati*. The second and third presses yield a less fatty coconut milk. In U.S. markets you now can choose from many forms of ready-processed coconut milk and cream: fresh in a ripe coconut, frozen, powdered, in a milk carton, and canned. After standing on a shelf awhile, the canned coconut separates into a thick top layer of cream and a bottom layer of milk. By opening the can gently and scooping out the thick layer, you can obtain coconut cream; or by shaking the can before opening, you will get coconut milk.

DURIAN: This spiky, brown, clublike, dark, aged-looking fruit is an acquired taste. Its strong, unique aroma and taste make it at once a forbidden delicacy and formidably expensive fruit, accessible to only the affluent. Nowadays, with advanced methods of cultivation, the fruit comes in many varieties, ranging in grade and price. The sweet, nutty, creamy taste of durian deserves a fair trial before being dismissed. A first timer should try a durian not fully ripe because it is less pungent in aroma and taste. The taste of a ripe durian is one-of-a-kind experience.

JACKFRUIT: *Kanon* is a brownish green fruit with short spiky skin. Its meat is a brilliant yellow or orange and has a unique, sweet flavor. Jackfruit is often used in Thai desserts because of its neutral sweetness that goes with anything. In the United States, you can readily find canned jackfruit in syrup in Asian grocery stores.

LONGAN: *Lumyai* has been cultivated for centuries as the cash crop in the cool North region. Longan fruit is round, the size of a cherry, with leathery brown skin, and has a very sweet flavor and strong, unique aroma. It can be eaten fresh or as a main ingredient for the dessert longan. In the United States, imported canned longan can be found year-round. Fresh longan can be found seasonally in well-stocked Asian markets.

LYCHEE: This fruit originated in China but has also been cultivated in the North of Thailand and has become a local fruit. Lychee fruit is round, a little bit bigger than a cherry, with red bumpy skin, and has a sweet flavor with a pleasant sour hint. In the United States, imported canned lychee can be found year-round. Fresh lychee can be found seasonally in well-stocked Asian markets.

MANGO: *Mamoung* in Thailand comes in more than seventy different sizes, shapes, and flavors. In Thai markets, there are always mangoes year-round, with different seasonal varieties. Mangoes are eaten both as a ripe fruit and in desserts, and unripe green mango is found in various salads and is prized for its sour taste. In the United States, only two kinds of mango are widely available. Mexican mango is almost round with red skin and, when ripe, has a sweet taste with a pleasant sour hint. Manila mango is flatter than the Mexican variety and has a pale yellow skin, custard-like texture, and a truly sweet taste.

MUNG BEAN: *Thua Leang* or *Thua Kiew* are yellow and green respectively and are often used in Thai desserts. The beans are sold mostly prepackaged in dried form.

POMELO: *Som Oo* is the giant grapefruit now readily available in almost all Asian markets in late winter. It is sweeter and less bitter than the local grapefruit, and eaten either as a fruit or as a main ingredient in salad.

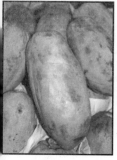

PAPAYA: *Malagor* is usually eaten ripe as fresh fruit, but unripe, green papaya is very popular for the Thai green papaya salad. Choose a papaya that is very hard and firm with bright green color. Peel and seed the papaya before shredding into fine pieces. In the United States, you may find the green papaya, which is imported from Mexico in well-stocked Asian grocery stores.

RAMBUTAN: *Ngor* has distinctive red hairy skin with opaque sweet white meat. It is imported seasonally from the Asia. However, *ngor* canned in syrup is also readily available.

STAR FRUIT: *Mafueng* in cross-section looks like a star, with light green skin and juicy meat. Star fruit has a mild sweet and sour taste and absorbs other flavors well in salads. It is often sweetened and sold as a dried fruit.

RICE, NOODLES, and WRAPPERS

A Thai meal can't be completed without a starch, which comes in many forms depending on region and type of meal. Thailand is the world's largest rice exporter. Rice, *Khao*, is served with almost every meal and is variously categorized. In general, *Khao* is the term Thai people call a complete meal. A specific type of rice, such as steamed rice *Khao Jao*, sticky rice *Khao Neaw*, or fried rice *Khao Pad* can be selected to accompany the meal. Rice is also processed into flour and processed further into noodles, wrappers, and other forms of starch. In addition to rice, mung beans or soybeans are also processed into many varieties of tofu, noodles, and wrappers.

FLOUR: *Paeng* is often used for making noodles and desserts and is named by its grain.

> **Rice Flour,** *Paeng Khao Jao*, is made from regular long-grain nonglutinous rice.

> **Glutinous Rice Flour,** *Paeng Khao Neaw*, is made from sweet or glutinous rice.

> **Corn Flour or Cornstarch,** *Paeng Khao Phot*, is very fine white flour made from corn.

> **Wheat Flour,** *Paeng Sali* or all-purpose flour, is made from wheat.

> **Tapioca Flour,** *Paeng Mun Sampalang*, is made from tapioca or cassava.

NOODLE: *Kuai-Tiao* is a Chinese word adopted by Thais to mean noodles or meals with noodles. There are many varieties of noodle, differing in size, shape, and also ingredients used in their production. In the United States, you can buy fresh sheets, and wide- or medium-size rice noodles in well-stocked

Asian grocery stores. Dried noodles are readily available in all sizes and qualities. Dried noodles should be soaked or boiled in water to soften.

Kuai-Tiao Sen Yai, 1-inch-wide rice noodles, are made from rice flour.

Kuai-Tiao Sen Lek, are 1/4-inch medium-wide rice noodles.

Kuai-Tiao Sen Mee, are fine-thread, small rice noodles.

Kanom Jeen, vermicelli rice noodles, are thin round noodles, made from freshly ground rice flour and sold in small portions that resemble bird's nests. *Kanom Jeen* is popular with many varieties of curry soup. In the United States, fresh noodles are difficult to find. The closest substitute is dried Japanese somen, which are also sold in well-stocked Asian grocery stores. Cook the noodles in boiling water until soft, drain, and rinse with cold water before portioning into small bird's nest-size wads.

Bami, egg noodles, are small yellow noodles made from flour and eggs. You can buy the noodles fresh in well-stocked Asian grocery stores. Dried egg noodles are also sold prepackaged in small balls. Cook the noodles in boiling water until soft.

Woon Sen, cellophane noodles or glass noodles, are made from mung bean flour. They often come in dry vermicelli threads. After being soaked or cooked in water, they turn clear, hence the name.

The Best of Regional Thai Cuisine

RICE: Khao Jao is the steamed white long-grain rice, which accompanies almost every meal in the Central and South regions.

Khao Hoam Mali, jasmine rice or fragrant rice, is extremely popular and available almost everywhere. Cook the rice in a pot with lid at a 1:2 1/2 ratio of dried rice to cold water. Before cooking, rinse the rice with water to cleanse away dirt and foreign objects. Bring the right mixture of rice and water to a boil and reduce the heat to simmer. Cover and continue cooking for 15 to 20 minutes until the water has been absorbed. Turn off the heat and let the rice steam for another 10 to 15 minutes before serving. After being cooked, rice becomes soft, fluffy and translucent and double in volume. If using a rice cooker, follow the manufacturer's instructions.

Khao Neaw, glutinous rice, sweet rice, or sticky rice, is the steamed medium-grain rice and the main staple in the North and Northeast regions. After being cooked, its texture becomes uniquely sticky, soft, and is easily shaped into a ball. It has a mild sweet flavor. Uncooked grains are whiter, shorter, and rounder than jasmine rice. The best way to cook the rice is to soak it overnight or at least 3 hours in cold water at a 1:3 ratio of rice and water, and then steam it with high heat in a steamer.

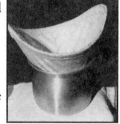

steamer

Khao Neaw Dum, black glutinous rice, is another variety of rice that has dark purple grains and a unique fragrance. It takes even longer to cook than its white counterpart.

TAPIOCA PEARLS: *Saku* are made from tapioca flour into round, different size balls: small, medium, and large. They are kneaded with lukewarm water to make dough or cooked in boiling water to make pudding.

TOFU: *Tao Hou* is widely available both in Japanese silky and Chinese firm textures. In a well-stocked Asian market you can also find special varieties of tofu, some with unique flavors and appearances simulating various meat products. Pre-fried tofu is also available and often used for its ability to absorb sauce well and to hold stuffing.

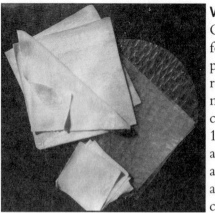

WRAPPERS: Thai cooking borrows many Chinese ingredients, especially its wrappers for many dishes. Certain varieties of wrapper help speed the cooking process. Spring roll wrappers and lumpia wrappers are made from flour dough and generally come in three sizes: 5-inch, 9-inch, and 12-inch squares. They are available fresh and frozen. The larger size can be cut according to your use. Wonton wrappers are made from flour and egg dough and come in two thicknesses: very thin for deep-frying, and thick for steaming or for making dumplings.

SAUCES and CONDIMENTS

In a Thai kitchen, there are few items besides rice that are a must to have for their authentic flavor. Most of these items are ready-made and available in convenient packages for U.S. markets. Most of them can be used alone or mixed with other ingredients, such as in fish sauce, and can last a long time with or without refrigeration. Your pantry for Thai cooking should be stocked with the following items.

CHILI SAUCE AND SAUCES: *Nam Jim*, various sauces, are prepared Thai condiments, which can be used readily or mixed in a dish.

Nam Jim Giem Boi, Chinese white plum sauce, is mild sweet and sour syrup and used as a sauce for delicately flavored dishes, such as shrimp cakes and corn fritters.

Nam Jim Gai, sweet chili sauce, is sweet and sour with evidence of mild red chili chunks, and is a popular sauce in fried or barbecued chicken.

Namprik Dong, or Sambal Olek of Indonesia, is ground hot and sour red chili in a vinegar mixture. It is popular for adding a chili zest to a bowl of noodle soup and various sauces.

Namprik Pow, chili paste with soybean oil, is a sweet, mild and smoky chili sauce that is often used as a flavor enhancer in salad dressings and hot and sour soups.

Namprik Sriracha, Sriracha chili sauce, is a hot, sweet, and sour sauce that can add a spicy heat to any dish.

Photo: Sweet Chili Sauce–*Nam Jim Kai*, Sriracha Chili Sauce–*Nam Prik Sriracha,*
Chinese White Plum Sauce–*Nam Jim Giem Boi*, Hot Chili Sauce–*Nam Prik Dong* or Sambal Olek,
Chili Paste with Soybean Oil–*Nam Prik Pow*

CURRY PASTE: *Namprik Gaeng*, comes in many varieties, in small cans for one time use and in a big plastic tub for several uses and should be refrigerated after opening. Ready-made paste is convenient and saves time. But to all Thai food connoisseurs, a fresh curry paste made from scratch in a mortar and pestle is worth going through the trouble.

DRIED SHRIMP: *Goong Haeng*, are shrimp preserved with salt and then sun-dried. They have a strong, concentrated taste. Dried shrimp are an important ingredient in sauces, curries, and chili dips. Seal tightly and store in the refrigerator for a few months.

BEAN SAUCE: *Tow Jeaw*, is made with whole beans fermented with salt, sugar, and rice powder. It serves as an enhancer with a unique flavor. Fermented black beans are the closest substitute.

FISH SAUCE: *Nam Pla* is a source of saltiness and a flavor enhancer for almost every Thai dish. *Khao Kup Nam Pla*, rice with fish sauce, is the term the Thais use to describe the barest staple among the poorest people. Fish sauce is a pungent, amber, clear liquid derived from a brew of fish and/or shrimp fermented with salt. Fish sauce always has a spot on the table, either as is or mixed with sliced chilies and/or lime juice—*(Nam Pla Prik)*. In the United States, fish sauce comes in glass and plastic bottles under several brand names, ranging from a high to low quality. High quality fish sauce has a fine aroma and taste with the right amount of salt. The sauce can be stored with or without refrigerator for up to a year.

MAGGI SEASONING: *Maggi sauce* originated in Switzerland but is now popular throughout Southeast Asia. It serves as a secret flavor enhancer in most marinade recipes. A few drops can improve flavor drastically. Thai people use Maggi as a sauce for various kinds of meat, and it is very popular on breakfast eggs instead of salt. A similar product under the brand name of Golden Mountain Sauce is also available.

OYSTER SAUCE: *Nam Mun Hoi* is an oyster extract with sweetened soy sauce and is used mostly in vegetable stir-fry dishes. It comes in three differnt varieties: real oyster extract, imitation oyster flavored sauce, and vegetarian oyster sauce. It must be refrigerated after opening.

SHRIMP PASTE: *Kapi* is a pungent, violet, or dark brown paste made from salted shrimp that has been air-dried or sun dried and then ground into a fine paste. Shrimp paste is a flavor enhancer in most curry pastes and chili dips. Seal tightly to prevent the strong aroma from leaking and store in the refrigerator for up to six months. Do not confuse the shrimp paste with the shrimp bouillon as in soup base. They are different products.

SUGAR: *Nam Tan* is a general term for sugar including granulated and brown sugar, which is made from sugar cane or sugar beet.

Palm or Coconut Sugar, *Nam Tan Peep*, is made from the sap of coconut or palm trees. It has a distinctive flavor and fragrance and a pale light-brown color. In the United States, palm sugar is available as paste in glass bottles or as crystallized round discs in clear plastic wraps, available in most well stocked Asian grocery stores. Chop or grind into small chunks to measure before use.

SWEET SOY SAUCE: *Se-Iew Dum* is a thick, sweet, dark sauce made from soy sauce and molasses. It is often used for its dark color, thick texture, and sweetness instead of sugar.

Sweet Dark Soy Sauce–*Se-Iew Dum*,
Maggi Sauce,
Oyster Sauce–*Nam Mun Hoi*

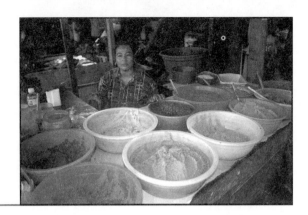

CURRY PASTES
and CHILI DIPS

Any complete Thai meal in any region includes a curry dish and/or chili dip. A mortar and pestle are used in every Thai kitchen for grinding. These days, for convenience and saving time, ready-made curry pastes are available in many varieties both in small cans and in large plastic tubs. They should be refrigerated after opening. But to all Thai food connoisseurs, a freshly made curry paste from scratch in a mortar and pestle is worth the trouble. The following article sums up all you need to know about making a curry or chili dip.

THAI CURRY and MORTAR:
The Cook's Disposition

Walking through my old neighborhood in central Thailand, I often hear different pounding rhythms from mortars and pestles. A lady of the house is preparing a curry paste to make a meal for her family. Some say that by observing the rhythm, one may be able to tell the cook's general disposition, her culinary taste, and her influence on the family. Some rhythms are short, with rapid beats in quick succession like a pistol, as the cook is perhaps short tempered and can easily blow her top. Other rhythms are long and firm, likened to a calm, solid individual. And yet others are sporadic and inconsistent, suggesting insecurity or perhaps just unfamiliarity with this cooking technique. Ever since I was young, when I made a paste, I would often use the mortar and pestle to release my anger and frustration. As we know, beating and pounding are effective in relieving tension. My family learned to notice my furious pounding and left me alone. Whatever the rhythm, the end result is a paste that reflects the taste preferences and, perhaps, the disposition of the cook who prepared it. Some pastes taste overly pungent, highlighting a particular spice that a short tempered cook would use, while others taste mellow and are well blended, showing the calm and solid nature of its cook. Some are inconsistent in their tastes, indicating that the cook needed more practice or security. Usually the tongue can tell, and in this case, the tongue and tune can tell tales and taste of the cook.

Mortar: Daily Life
and Heirloom

Thai people use *Krok* and *Saak*, the mortar and pestle, almost daily, to grind and mix herbs and spices in making various pastes for their meals. In this part of the world, we would probably switch to a high-tech blender or food processor. However, most Thai chefs will attest that a mortar and pestle produces far better chili and curry pastes because the grinding and pounding motion breaks down essences and oils from the ingredients better. A good mortar and pestle, along with secret recipes for curry pastes are handed down from mothers to daughters through many generations, and are considered a family heirloom. Some recipes secretly require marijuana buds or seeds for the paste grinding process. I was told to try one out in a restaurant in central Thailand during my last visit. The curry was fresh and sublimely delicious. I couldn't tell if the rumor was true, but I went back several times to this always-crowded restaurant to try their other varieties of curry and chili dishes.

Different Kinds of Mortar
for Different Tasks

Krok Din, clay mortar

There are two types of mortar and pestle, each serving a particular purpose: *Krok Hin*, stone mortar, and *Krok Din*, clay mortar. Aung Sila village in Cholburi province along the Gulf of Thailand is well known for its quality craftsmanship. It is situated in a mountain range of fine quality granite. The *krok hin* mortar (bowl) and *saak* (pestle) are made of solid granite and are hand-carved from a selected piece of the stone by *krok* artisans. The mortar is very heavy and sturdy and has a stubby shape; its mouth is wide and has a very thick rim. It's perfect for heavy pounding in making chili and curry pastes and is well guarded as an heirloom. I heard that its pestle could also be used as a weapon, like the frying pan, in extreme situations.

The word *Saak*, if being used as a Thai slang, constitutes a foul word for a promiscuous woman, who runs around pounding with different

Krok Hin, stone mortar

The Best of Regional Thai Cuisine

men. The granite mortar and pestle are long lasting and seldom break. I haven't yet seen any woman break the mortar. If one did and the news got out, the event would damage her reputation, leaving her acceptable only to an undesirable mate, or cursed for breaking up the family. To me, she would be considered a Bionic Woman or Super Girl!

Krok din is easily to make by hand. The mortar is made of clay and kiln fired and its pestle is carved out of wood. It is a lot less expensive than the *krok hin*, but has a shorter life and is disposable. I have successfully destroyed quite a few of these mortars. It is shaped like a tall cylinder, with a wide mouth and a narrow base. It is light, unstable, and not suitable for making pastes. Its main function is to serve as a mixing or tossing bowl, with little grinding. The famous Green Papaya Salad, *Som Tum* (pages 78 and 123), uses this kind of mortar to mix and toss its ingredients.

Curries and Chili Pastes for All Preferences

Thai curries have much Indian influence with such spices such as cumin and coriander. But Thais have added a number of local spices, including fresh and dried chilies, to create a variety of curries to call their own. The process of making a paste is not complicated, but is long and monotonous. It takes 20 to 30 minutes to grind ingredients into a smooth paste. Principal ingredients are garlic, shallots, chilies, lemongrass, galangal, kaffir lime, Indian spices, and a knockout pungent flavor enhancer, shrimp paste. Some of us can't stand the shrimp paste and have to live without it. The shrimp paste, in an uncooked stage, emits a very pungent aroma of fermented or rotten shrimp. After being cooked, its aroma and flavor are less pungent and more desirable.

Because of its abrasive smell, orchard growers often use the shrimp paste to repel wild monkeys that steal fruit and destroy tools. Shrimp paste is applied to the fruit trees and the tools; if monkeys come into contact, they rub and clean their fingers, in most cases, until they bleed. This painful lesson discourages them from coming near the trees and tools again.

Colors of chili also determine the kind of curry and heat intensity, such as the hot and sweet Green Curry, the pungent Red Curry, and the aromatic and mild *Panaeng*, or Yellow Curry. In my childhood, as the youngest of the family, I was often left with my aunt in the kitchen with a task of grinding paste, while my brothers and sisters ran off to play. You could tell that I hated it so much by the rhythm of my pounding, and by the taste because I sometimes added more chilies to the paste than the recipe called for. The result was usually an overly hot curry soup that no one wanted to eat. To teach me a lesson, I was forced to eat my own spicy creations.

Many well-established Thai restaurants prepare their own fresh chili and curry pastes. Their recipes vary from one place to another in the amount and proportion of each ingredient to create a well-balanced flavor. A good fresh paste makes a world difference in a curry soup. The most famous Thai curry dishes in the United States are Green Curry *Keow Wan* and the *Panaeng* curry. It is such a satisfying, self-indulgent experience to have a smoldering aromatic curry soup with hot steamed rice. Both dishes use coconut milk for a creamy base. But don't despair if you're not a coconut lover. Many Thai chili and curry dishes are prepared without coconut, such as Fish Cake *Tod Mon*, Red Curry fish or chicken *Pad Ped*, Hunter Soup *Gaeng Paa*, or Sour Soup *Gaeng Som*. For your convenience, all curry pastes come prepackaged and ready to be used. This makes for convenience, but you can't control the heat intensity of the chili, which is often inconsistent, not to mention the preservatives in the ingredients. I prefer making my own fresh paste, so may you, and you can also modify a recipe to suit your taste.

Chili in Vinegar

10 whole green and red peppers, *prik chee fa*,
serrano, or jalapeño
3/4 cup distilled vinegar

Preparation: Slice the peppers into thin rings. Combine all ingredients.

Fish Sauce with Chili

1/4 cup fish sauce
1/4 cup lime juice
2 tablespoons chopped chili, bird's-eye, serrano, or
jalapeño
1 tablespoon granulated sugar (optional)
1 teaspoon chopped garlic (optional)

Preparation: Combine all ingredients.

Gaeng Koa Curry Paste

Makes 1 cu

6 to 10 whole dried large red chilies, *prik chee fa*,
    serrano, jalapeño, or California chili
2 tablespoons chopped shallot
2 tablespoons chopped garlic
2 tablespoons chopped lemongrass, tender part
1 tablespoon chopped galangal
1 teaspoon chopped kaffir lime skin or leaf
1 teaspoon whole black pepper
1 teaspoon shrimp paste
1 teaspoon salt

Preparation: Seed the dried chilies and then soak in warm water until soft. Drain and squeeze dry.

Grind and pound all ingredients in a mortar with pestle, putting in one ingredient at a time, until they form a smooth paste.

If using a blender or food processor, combine all ingredients and blend until they form a smooth paste, adding some oil to help blending.

Gaeng Som Curry Paste

Namprik Gaeng Som

Makes 1 cup

6 to 10 whole dried large red chilies, *prik chee fa*,
   serrano, jalapeño, or California chili
3 tablespoons chopped shallot
2 tablespoons chopped garlic
2 tablespoons chopped galangal
1/4 cup chopped lesser ginger, *krachai*
1 tablespoon chopped kaffir lime skin or leaf
1 tablespoon chopped lemongrass, tender part
2 teaspoons shrimp paste
1 teaspoon salt

Preparation: Seed the dried chilies and then soak in warm water until soft. Drain and squeeze dry.

Grind and pound all ingredients in a mortar with pestle, putting in one ingredient at a time until they form a smooth paste.

If using a blender or food processor, combine all ingredients and blend until they form a smooth paste, adding some oil to help blending.

Green Curry Paste

    5 whole fresh large green chilies, *prik chee fa,*
        serrano, or jalapeño
    10 whole fresh green bird's-eye chilies
    3 tablespoons chopped fresh lemongrass, tender part
    3 tablespoons chopped shallot
    2 tablespoons chopped garlic
    1 tablespoon chopped fresh galangal
    1 tablespoon chopped cilantro roots or stems
    1 teaspoon cumin seeds, more to taste
    2 teaspoons coriander seeds, more to taste
    1 teaspoon whole black pepper
    1 teaspoon chopped kaffir lime skin or leaves
    1 teaspoon salt
    1 teaspoon shrimp paste

Preparation: Arrange all ingredients on a baking tray and roast in a 375°F oven until fragrant, about 7 to 10 minutes. Let cool.

Grind and pound all ingredients in a mortar with pestle, putting in one ingredient at a time, until they form a smooth paste.

If using a blender or food processor, combine all ingredients and process until they form a smooth paste, adding some oil to help blending.

Hunter (Gaeng Paa) Curry Paste *Namprik Gaeng Paa*

Makes 1 cup

6 to 10 whole dried large red chilies, *prik chee fa*,
serrano, jalapeño, or California chili
1 teaspoon whole black pepper
2 teaspoons coriander seeds, more to taste
3 tablespoons chopped shallot
2 tablespoons chopped garlic
3 tablespoons chopped lemongrass, tender part
2 tablespoons chopped galangal
1 tablespoon chopped kaffir lime skin or leaf
1 teaspoon salt
1 teaspoon shrimp paste

Preparation: Seed the dried red chilies and soak in warm water until soft. Drain and squeeze dry.

Roast the pepper and coriander in a pan over a stove or in a 375°F oven until fragrant, about 7 to 10 minutes.

Grind and pound all ingredients in a mortar with pestle, putting in one ingredient at a time, until they form a smooth paste.

If using a blender or food processor, combine all ingredients and blend until they form a smooth paste, add some oil to help blending.

Massamun Curry Paste

Namprik Gaeng Massamun

Makes 1 cup

6 to 10 whole dried large red chilies, *prik chee fa,*
   serrano, jalapeño, or California chili
2 teaspoons coriander seeds
2 teaspoons cumin seeds
1 teaspoon cardamom seeds
1 teaspoon whole black pepper
3 tablespoons chopped shallot
2 tablespoons chopped garlic
2 tablespoons chopped lemongrass, tender part
1 tablespoon chopped galangal
1 tablespoon chopped cilantro root or stem
2 teaspoons chopped kaffir lime skin or leaves
1 tablespoon ground nutmeg
1 teaspoon ground cinnamon
1 teaspoon salt
2 teaspoons shrimp paste

Preparation: Seed the dried red chilies and soak in warm water until soft. Drain and squeeze dry.

Roast the coriander, cumin, cardamom, and black pepper in a pan over a stove or in a 375°F oven until fragrant, about 7 to 10 minutes.

Grind and pound all ingredients in a mortar with pestle, putting in one ingredient at a time, until they form a smooth paste.

If using a blender or food processor, combine all ingredients and process until they form a smooth paste, adding some oil to help blending.

Panaeng Curry Paste

6 to 10 whole dried large red chilies, *prik chee fa*,
   serrano, jalapeño, or California chili
2 teaspoons coriander seeds, more to taste
1 teaspoons cumin seeds, more to taste
2 tablespoons chopped shallot
2 tablespoons chopped garlic
2 tablespoons chopped lemongrass, tender part
1 tablespoon chopped galangal
1 tablespoon chopped kaffir lime skin or leaves
1 tablespoon chopped cilantro root or stem
2 teaspoons shrimp paste
1 teaspoon salt

Preparation: Seed the dried red chilies and soak in warm water until soft. Drain and squeeze dry.

Roast the coriander and cumin seeds in a pan over a stove or in a 375°F oven until fragrant, about 7 to 10 minutes.

Grind and pound all ingredients in a mortar with pestle, putting in one ingredient at a time, until they form a smooth paste.

If using a blender or food processor, combine all ingredients and process until they form a smooth paste, adding some oil to help blending.

Red Curry Paste

10 to 15 whole dried large red chilies, *prik chee fa,*
serrano, jalapeño, or California chili
2 teaspoons coriander seeds, more to taste
1 teaspoon cumin seeds, more to taste
2 tablespoons chopped red bird's-eye chilies (optional fo
more heat)
2 tablespoons chopped shallot
2 tablespoons chopped garlic
2 tablespoons chopped lemongrass, tender part
1 tablespoon chopped galangal
1 tablespoon chopped kaffir lime skin or leaves
1 tablespoon chopped cilantro roots or stems
1 teaspoon salt
2 teaspoons shrimp paste

Preparation: Seed the dried chilies and then soak in warm water until soft.
Drain and squeeze dry.

Roast the coriander and cumin seeds in a pan over a stove or in a 375°F oven
until fragrant, about 7 to 10 minutes.

Grind and pound all ingredients in a mortar with pestle, putting in one ingredient at a time, until they form a smooth paste.

If using a blender or food processor, combine all ingredients and process unti
they form a smooth paste, adding some oil to help blending.

Shrimp Paste Chili Dip

1 tablespoon shrimp paste
1 banana leaf (optional)
1 tablespoon chopped garlic
5 whole chopped bird's-eye chilies,
    more or less to taste
2 whole chopped Thai round eggplants, *makheua pro*
2 tablespoons fish sauce, more to taste
3 tablespoons lime juice, more to taste
1 tablespoon palm sugar

Preparation: Wrap the shrimp paste in the banana leaf or aluminum foil and roast in a 375°F oven or on a fire grill until heated through and fragrant, about 7 to 10 minutes.

In a mortar with pestle, grind the shrimp paste with garlic until roughly ground. Add the chilies and eggplants; grind to small chunks.

Stir in the fish sauce, lime juice, and palm sugar; mix well.

Serve the chili dip as a sauce for fried or steamed fish or serve it with fresh and cooked vegetables.

Steamed Mackerel (*Pla Too*)

Southern Yellow Curry Paste   *Namprik Gaeng Leaung*

Makes 1/2 cup

12 whole dried red bird's-eye chilies
10 whole chopped fresh yellow bird's-eye chilies
3 tablespoons chopped shallot
1/4 cup chopped lesser ginger, *kra chai*
2 tablespoons chopped fresh turmeric or powder
1 teaspoon chopped galangal
1 teaspoon salt
2 tablespoons shrimp paste

Preparation: Chop the dried chili and soak in warm water until soft. Drain and squeeze dry.

Grind and pound all ingredients in a mortar with pestle, putting in one ingredient at a time, until they form a smooth paste.

If using a blender or food processor, combine all ingredients and process until they form a smooth paste, adding some oil to help blending.

Southern Tai Pla Curry Paste

Namprik Gaeng Tai Pla

Makes 1/2 cup

25 whole dried red bird's-eye chilies
1 tablespoon chopped shallot
3 tablespoons chopped garlic
3 tablespoons chopped lemongrass, tender part
1 tablespoon chopped galangal
2 tablespoons chopped kaffir lime skin or leaf
2 teaspoons peeled and chopped fresh turmeric
2 teaspoons shrimp paste
1 teaspoon salt

Preparation: Chop the dried chilies and then soak in warm water until soft. Drain and squeeze dry.

Grind and pound all ingredients in a mortar with pestle, putting in one ingredient at a time, until they form a smooth paste.

If using a blender or food processor, combine all ingredients and process until they form a smooth paste, adding some oil to help blending.

Yellow Curry Paste

Namprik Gaeng Kari

Makes 1 cup

8 to 12 whole dried large red chilies, *prik chee fa*,
  serrano, jalapeño, or California chili
2 teaspoons coriander seeds, more to taste
1 teaspoon cumin seeds, more to taste
2 tablespoons chopped shallot
2 tablespoons chopped garlic
3 tablespoons chopped lemongrass, tender part
2 tablespoons chopped galangal
1 teaspoon chopped ginger
2 teaspoons chopped kaffir lime skin or leaf
1 tablespoon curry powder, more to taste
1 teaspoon salt

Preparation: Seed the dried chilies and then soak in warm water until soft. Drain and squeeze dry.

Roast the coriander and cumin seeds in a pan over a stove or in a 375° oven until fragrant, about 7 to 10 minutes.

Grind and pound all ingredients in a mortar with pestle, putting in one ingredient at a time, until they form a smooth paste.

If using a blender or food processor, combine all ingredients and process until they form a smooth paste, adding some oil to help blending.

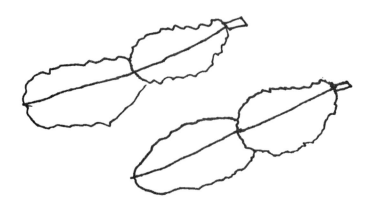

Young Chili Dip

10 whole young bird's-eye chilies, serranos, or jalapeños
1/4 cup chopped shallot
1/4 cup chopped garlic
1 cup chopped unripe tomato, seeded
2 tablespoons chopped anchovy
1 banana leaf (optional)
2 tablespoons fish sauce, more to taste
2 tablespoons lime juice, more to taste
2 tablespoons palm sugar

Preparation: Spread the chili, shallot, garlic, tomato, and anchovy on a tray. Roast in a 375°F oven until fragrant, about 7 to 10 minutes. Or wrap in banana leaf or aluminum foil and roast over a fire grill until fragrant, about 7 to 10 minutes.

In a mortar with pestle or food processor, process all ingredients until well mixed.

Serve the chili dip with fresh and cooked vegetables or serve it as a sauce for fried or steamed fish.

North
Lum Tae

Mountains and Cool Climate

A legend of the North has it that there was once a young maiden who was very fond of eating Thai eggplants, *Ma-Kheua*. There was also an unfortunate peasant named San Pomp, "ten thousand bumps" for the skin disease he had, which covered his entire body with bumps and boils.

San Pomp was a farmer, who grew an eggplant tree near the stairway leading up to his hut. For convenience, his way of watering and fertilizing the plant was to urinate on the tree. His eggplant tree thrived and produced the biggest and most beautiful eggplants in the area.

Somehow, his eggplants were selected for the royal kitchen and ended up on the princess' dinner plate. Not long after consuming the eggplants, the princess became pregnant by an unknown father and later delivered a very beautiful little prince. The princess' father, the king, exhausted his means trying to find the father of his grandson. He finally organized a matchmaking ceremony. He asked that any man in the area who might be father to the little prince bring a food offering to the boy. The king prayed for God's help in guiding the little prince to accept only food from his real father's hand.

During the ceremony, many men who wished to become the king's son-in-law brought all sorts of foods elaborately prepared with the finest, most delicious ingredients to entice the little prince, alas, to no avail. The prince accepted from no one, until finally, the ugly San Pomp brought in a cold leftover lump of sticky rice—a staple in the North—and offered it to the prince. To everyone's surprise, the little prince accepted and ate the food from San Pomp's hand.

The king was so embarrassed by his son-in-law and angry with his daughter, that he deported his only blood relative and San Pomp out of his kingdom. San Pomp and his family wandered in extreme hardship throughout the land, ignorant of almighty God above, until mercifully, God came down and granted San Pomp three wishes. His first wish, to become a handsome man, was granted. For his second wish, he asked for his own kingdom and that he would rule it as a king. And for the last wish, he asked for a gold crib for his son. As legend would have it, his son became the mighty king of the North—king Ou Tong, "the Golden Crib."

Geographically embraced by the Tanow Wasri rugged ridge of mountains, 8,445 feet at its peak, the North has a pleasant cool climate compared to the hot and humid southern regions. The mountains form a natural border to Burma (Myanmar) and Laos, situated in the infamous Golden Triangle. The mountains slope down into the fertile Northern rolling plateau, creating four sister rivers: the Ping, the Wung, the Yom, and the Nan, which flow into the mighty Chao Praya River in central Thailand.

Though Thais in general are quite mellow, adhering to the Thai motto *"Sabuy Sabuy"* meaning "whatever," I have found Thais in the North to be extremely *Sabuy Sabuy*. The mellow disposition and peaceful way of life have been shaped by the temperate climate and fertile land; the Thais in the North have seldom had to face economic hardship. Their crafts, architecture, language, cuisine, and conduct are the highlight of Thai civilization.

I may describe the Northern people as mellow, but the pungent spices and chili pastes in their cuisine run counter to their mild disposition. The neighboring countries of Myanmar and Laos influence their culinary tradition. *Gaeng Hung Lay* is a popular Burmese-influenced curry dish, as well as *Khoa Soi*, the signature dish of the North. Not less distinctive, the Laotian-influenced *Khao Neaw*, or sticky rice, is the staple, instead of the soft, boiled rice or jasmine rice of the Central and South regions. *Namprik*, a basic element in every meal, is a chili dip or sauce accompanied by fresh or cooked vegetables. *Namprik* ranges in heat intensity, from the mild *Namprik Ong*, minced pork with tomato and spice mixture, to the fiery *Namprik Tadaeng*, dried red chili with spices and

The Best of Regional Thai Cuisine

shrimp paste.

The cool climate of the North annually produces a unique fruit that grows only in this region: *Lumyai*, known as *Longan* throughout the world. *Longan* plays an important role in Northern desserts, both as a fresh fruit and for its unique flavor and texture in sweet rice pudding, syrup, and beverages.

The Northern hospitality is showcased in a traditional feast called *Khun Toke*. *Khun Toke* is a classical style of dinner offering especially for important guests or dignitaries. A round 2-foot-tall table with upward rim is constructed or carved out of wood then polished, decorated, and lacquered. Several dishes of food are arranged on this table and served in front of the guests who sit on the floor. The meal consists typically of Northern delicacies such as *Gaeng Hung Lay*, a curry dish, *Gaeng Hoa*, a soup made from various vegetables, *Namprik Ong*, chicken salad, pork rinds, sausages, rice puff, fresh vegetables, and *Nam Ton* for beverage. Accompaniments are a woven bamboo container, *kratip*, full with sticky rice, a bowl of water for rinsing hands, and hand-rolled local cigarettes called *Khee Yo*. The mouthwatering feast seldom goes without a feast for the eyes. Northern classical dances and music are performed throughout the meal.

This version of well-seasoned marinated beef stands out from that of other regions because of its sugar and coriander spice. It can be eaten as a snack or with sticky rice as a meal and is popular as an accompaniment to curries and chili dips. The combination of beef and sticky rice is a convenient and delicious meal suitable for a picnic or to take on a trip.

1 pound beef, flat or flank steak
1 teaspoon ground coriander
1 tablespoon very finely minced cilantro root or stem
2 tablespoons fish sauce
2 tablespoons Maggi seasoning
3 tablespoons brown sugar
2 cups vegetable oil for frying

Preparation: Slice the beef into thin, long strips.

Combine all ingredients *except* the oil and marinate the beef for at least 1 hou

On a tray lined with wax paper, arrange the beef strips and place in a drafty spot to dry for at least 2 hours or until the liquid is evaporated. Or bake in an oven at 200°F until dry, about 15 to 20 minutes.

In a deep pan over medium heat, heat the oil to 350° to 375°F and fry the beef in small batches until done, 5 to 7 minutes. Fry longer if you prefer them crispy. The beef can also be grilled for less oil.

Drain on absorbent papers and serve as a snack or serve with sticky rice as a main course.

Barbecued Chicken Wings

There is no other way to make chicken wings so appealing, delicious, and healthy as this barbecue recipe. Overnight marinating helps the herb and spice flavors to infiltrate through each molecule of the wing. Charcoal grilling provides a hint of smokiness and striking black charred marks against the golden wings. You may find eating with your fingers, tearing the meat from the bones, to be a fun experience that puts you in touch with your primal instinct.

> 3 tablespoons chopped garlic
> 1/2 cup chopped lemongrass, tender part
> 1/4 cup chopped cilantro root or stem
> 2 teaspoons ground turmeric
> 1 teaspoon ground white pepper
> 1 tablespoon granulated sugar
> 1 teaspoon salt
> 2 pounds chicken wings, cleaned, and trimmed

Preparation: In a mortar with pestle or food processor, process the garlic, lemongrass, cilantro, turmeric, pepper, sugar, and salt until they form a smooth paste.

Marinate the chicken wings overnight or at least 6 hours.

Prepare charcoals at least 30 minutes ahead of time for medium coals. Barbecue the wings for 6 to 8 minutes on each side until done and golden brown.

Serve the wings with chili dips (pages 31 and 43) or Thai Sweet Chili Sauce (see glossary) as a snack or serve with sticky rice as a main course.

Barbecued Pork

Pork is a popular choice of meat in Northern cuisine. This is the easiest way to prepare it, using four basic seasonings for the paste: garlic, cilantro or coriander, pepper, and salt or fish sauce. Charcoal grilling over an open flame intensifies the flavors of all the ingredients and adds smoky essence and an appetizing charred appearance. A sweet hint of smoked coconut in the marinade invites a mouthwatering feast.

> 1 pound pork loin
> 2 tablespoons chopped garlic
> 2 tablespoons chopped cilantro root or stem
> 1 tablespoon ground coriander
> 1 teaspoon ground white pepper
> 3 tablespoons granulated sugar
> 1 cup coconut cream
> 3 tablespoons fish sauce
> 2 tablespoons Maggi seasoning
> 1 package bamboo skewers (optional), soaked in water

Preparation: Slice the pork into 1/2 x 5-inch thin strips.

In a mortar with pestle or food processor, process the garlic, cilantro, coriander, and pepper until they form a smooth paste.

In a bowl, combine the pork, paste, sugar, coconut cream, fish sauce, and Maggi seasoning. Stir to mix well and marinate for at least 2 hours. The pork strips can be skewered on bamboo sticks for an easy handling.

Prepare charcoals at least 30 minutes ahead of time for medium coals and barbecue the pork for 3 to 5 minutes on each side until done and golden brown.

Serve the pork with chili dips (pages 31 and 43) or Thai Sweet Chili Sauce (see glossary) as a snack or serve with sticky rice as a main course.

Beef Burmese Curry

Pad Ped Neua Burma

Next door to the North is Burma or Myanmar, whose descendents in Thailand are called *"Thai Yai,"* Big Thai. Thai people in comparison to *Thai Yai* are called *"Thai Noi,"* Little Thai, and the northern Thais are called *"Thai Lanna,"* named for an ancient kingdom of the north. This Burmese recipe has also been influenced by neighboring India in its use of spices. By the time this dish reached Thailand, it had been incorporated as one of the local fusion dishes.

Chili Paste
8 whole dried large red chilies, *prik chee fa*, serrano, jalapeño, or California chili
2 tablespoons chopped shallot
1 tablespoon chopped garlic
2 tablespoons chopped lemongrass, tender part
1 teaspoon chopped galangal
2 whole cloves
1 teaspoon ground turmeric
2 tablespoons ground cumin
1/2 teaspoon ground cinnamon
1 teaspoon shrimp paste

Preparation: Seed and soak the chilies in warm water until soft. Drain and squeeze dry. In a mortar with pestle or food processor, process all ingredients until they form a smooth paste; set aside.

3 tablespoons butter
1 pound beef sirloin, diced into 1-inch cubes
3 tablespoons fish sauce
1 tablespoon granulated sugar (optional)
1/4 cup sliced shallot or red onion
1 tablespoon chopped young ginger

Preparation: In a pot over medium heat, add the butter and cook the chili paste until fragrant. Stir in the beef and cook until done about 5 minutes.

Add 1/2 cup water and fish sauce. Continue cooking until the beef is tender, about 7 minutes. Stir in the sugar, if using, shallot, and ginger. Remove from the heat and serve.

Curried Noodles

Every region has its own version of this dish, but the North prepares it with pork and beef instead of fish, and even gives it the strange name of Nam Gnew, which means the noodles of opium growers. It is available inexpensively almost everywhere in the North and is served with an array of fresh and preserved vegetables as accompaniments. When you haven't decided what to eat, this dish may appear conveniently right before your eyes, either at a sidewalk hawker's stand or from a wandering merchant.

Chili Paste
8 whole dried large red chilies, *prik chee fa*, serrano, jalapeño, or California chili
1 tablespoon chopped garlic
2 tablespoons chopped shallot
1 teaspoon chopped galangal
1 tablespoon chopped lemongrass, tender part
1 teaspoon chopped cilantro root or stem
1 tablespoon ground turmeric
1 teaspoon salt
1 teaspoon shrimp paste

Preparation: Seed and soak the chilies in warm water until soft. Drain and squeeze dry. In a mortar with pestle or food processor, process all ingredients until they form a smooth paste; set aside.

1/4 cup vegetable oil
2 tablespoons very thinly sliced garlic, for garnish
1/2 pound ground lean pork
1/2 pound ground lean beef
1/2 pound chopped cherry tomatoes
1 tablespoon minced fermented bean sauce
  or black beans
2 tablespoons fish sauce
8 ounces dried rice vermicelli or Japanese somen
1/4 cup chopped cilantro and green onion for garnish
1/2 cup thinly sliced pickled Chinese mustard greens,
  for accompaniment
1 pound bean sprouts for accompaniment
2 whole limes, cut in wedges for accompaniment
2 tablespoons chili flakes for accompaniment

Preparation: In a pot over medium heat, heat the oil and cook the garlic until light brown and crispy. Strain and set aside for garnish.

With the same oil, stir in the chili paste and cook until fragrant. Add the pork and beef and break down into small chunks.

Add the tomatoes, 1/4 cup water, bean sauce, and fish sauce. Stir to mix well and simmer for 15 minutes until all ingredients are well integrated.

Cook the noodles in boiling water until tender. Drain and rinse in cold water. Let dry and portion into small wads, each about the size of a small bird's nest.

To serve, arrange a couple of wads of noodles on serving plates and top with a generous amount of the curry. Garnish with the fried garlic, cilantro, and green onion. Serve with the accompaniments.

Curried Egg Noodles

Khao Soi, a signature dish of the North, means shredded rice, as the production process involves making rice into thin sheets and slicing or shredding the sheets into flat noodles. Chinese flat egg noodles are the best substitute and are easy to find. Fresh ginger in the chili paste gives this noodle a unique flavor, differing from other noodle dishes.

Chili Paste
8 whole dried large red chilies, *prik chee fa*, serrano, jalapeño, or California chili
3 tablespoons chopped shallot
2 tablespoons chopped ginger
1 tablespoon ground coriander
1 tablespoon ground turmeric
1 teaspoon salt

Preparation: Seed and soak the chilies in warm water until soft. Drain and squeeze dry. In a mortar with pestle or food processor, process all ingredients until they form a smooth paste; set aside.

5 1/2 cups coconut milk
1 pound chicken thigh meat, diced into 1/2-inch cubes
1/2 teaspoon salt
1/4 cup light soy sauce
2 tablespoons dark sweet soy sauce
10 ounces dried flat egg noodles
1/4 cup vegetable oil
2 tablespoons chili flakes
1 cup sliced red onion for accompaniment
2 cups pickled Chinese mustard greens
    for accompaniment

Preparation: In a pot over medium heat, add 1/2 cup of the coconut milk. Stir in the chili paste and cook until fragrant.

Stir in the chicken and cook until done. Add the remaining 5 cups coconut milk, the salt, and soy sauces. Continue cooking until the chicken is tender for 10 minutes. Do not let it boil over.

Fry 1 cup of the dried noodles in hot oil until golden brown and crispy. Remove and set aside to drain. Fry the chili flakes in the same hot oil and reserve both chili and oil.

Cook the remaining unfried dry noodles in boiling water until tender. Drain and rinse in cold water.

To serve, place the noodles on serving plates and top with a generous amount of the curry. Garnish with the crispy noodles. Serve with the chili oil and accompaniments.

Hung Lay Curry

This popular dish is Burmese-influenced but still maintains its Thai characteristics in many Northern secret family recipes. A slow-cook method is used to prepare pork and beef in coconut milk and curry paste. Most of the recipes favor pork with layers of skin, fat, and lean meat, which give full flavor, yet are less expensive. Beef can be used, if you prefer. This complex-flavored dish with its mouth-watering meat is served with steamed sticky rice.

Curry Paste
10 whole dried red chilies, *prik chee fa*, serrano,
  jalapeño, or California chili
3 tablespoons chopped garlic
2 tablespoons chopped shallot
1/4 cup chopped lemongrass, tender part
2 tablespoons chopped ginger
1 teaspoon shrimp paste

Preparation: Seed the dried chilies and then soak in warm water until soft. Drain and squeeze dry.

Process all ingredients in a mortar with pestle, putting in one ingredient at a time, until they form a smooth paste. If using a blender or food processor, combine all ingredients and blend, adding some oil to help blending.

1/2 pound pork, diced into 1/2-inch cubes
1/2 pound beef (top or bottom round),
  diced 1/2-inch cubes
1/4 cup fish sauce
2 tablespoons sweet soy sauce
3 tablespoons palm sugar
2 1/2 cups coconut milk
1/4 cup tamarind liquid
1 tablespoon curry powder

Preparation: In a bowl, combine the pork, beef, fish sauce, soy sauce, and palm sugar. Marinate the meats for at least 30 minutes.

In a pot over medium heat, add 1/2 cup of the coconut milk. Stir in the chili paste and cook until fragrant.

Stir in the marinated meats and cook until well coated with the paste. Add the remaining 2 cups of the coconut milk, tamarind liquid, and curry powder.

Bring the mixture to a boil and reduce the heat to simmer. Continue cooking until the meats are tender and the liquid is absorbed, 20 to 30 minutes. The curry should be fairly thick with meats that melt in your mouth. Serve the Hung Lay Curry with sticky rice.

Pork and Ginger Sausage

This dish is considered a sausage, "Hnaem," but is prepared fresh and not stuffed into cases, unlike the other Northern sausages which need to be encased and fermented. The recipe uses shredded pork skin for its unique elastic yet crunchy texture, but it can be easily omitted to accommodate your taste. Lime helps cure the meat and provides a refreshing flavor. Fresh ginger adds a snappy, spicy zest to this well-balanced dish. Roasted peanuts and fresh vegetables, such as aromatic Chinese lettuce, are essential accompaniments. The lettuce leaves are also used as wrappers when eating the sausage.

1/4 pound pork skin, cleaned
3 tablespoons vegetable oil
5 whole dried red bird's-eye chilies
1/2 pound ground lean pork
1/4 cup fish sauce, more to taste
1/4 cup lime juice, more to taste
1 tablespoon granulated sugar (optional)
1 tablespoon finely minced garlic
1/4 cup finely shredded young ginger
1/4 cup finely sliced shallot or red onion
1 tablespoon minced bird's-eye chilies,
   more or less to taste
1/2 cup roasted peanuts for accompaniment
5 stalks green onion for accompaniment
1 head Chinese lettuce for accompaniment

Preparation: Poach the pork skin in boiling water until done for 15 minutes. Drain and slice into 2-inch-long, paper-thin strips; set aside.

In a pan over medium heat, add the oil and fry the dried chilies until crispy. Set aside for garnish.

a a pot over medium heat, bring 1/4 cup water to a boil. Stir in the ground
ork, break it down to small chunks, and cook until done. Remove from the
eat and let cool until lukewarm. Stir in the sliced pork skin.

dd the fish sauce, lime juice, sugar, garlic, ginger, shallot, and bird's-eye
uilies; gently toss to mix well. Transfer the mixture onto a serving platter and
arnish with fried chilies. Serve with all accompaniments.

This recipe calls for true sausages, which need time to ferment and develo a sour taste. The sour taste derives from cooked rice whose acidity helps cur and tenderize the pork. Let the meat ferment longer if you prefer a very sour sausage. It needs an accompaniment to bring out its true fermented flavors.

1 pound ground lean pork
1/2 cup shredded pork skin, 2-inch-long strips
1/2 cup steamed rice or sticky rice, mashed
1 1/2 teaspoons salt
8 whole bird's-eye chilies
1 tablespoon minced garlic
1/4 cup cornstarch
6 pieces banana leaves or 8 x 12-inch plastic bags
1 cup roasted peanuts for accompaniment
1/4 cup sliced fresh ginger for accompaniment
1 head Chinese or green leaf lettuce for accompanimen
6 stalks green onion for accompaniment
6 stalks mint leaves for accompaniment

Preparation: In a bowl, combine all ingredients *except* the banana leaves and accompaniments. Knead and mix the mixture until thoroughly well combin

Roll the sausage mixture into cylindrical shape, 1-inch diameter x 6-inch-lor pieces. Wrap the mixture in the banana leaves or plastic bags in several layers and tuck both ends tightly. Tie the wrapped sausages securely with strings or rubber bands.

Let the sausages marinate, cure, and set for 5 to 7 days in a cool spot or refriger tor. Acidity from the fermenting rice w cure the meat and provide the sour tast

To serve, unwrap the sausages and slice on a bias in thin pieces and serve with the accompaniments. The sausage can also be cooked by sautéing, steaming, o barbecuing.

Tomato and Pork Chili Dip *Namprik Ong*

Serves 6

This Northern signature dish offers a good balance of sweet and sour. The dish is part of almost every meal and is served with crispy pork rinds and a variety of fresh vegetables. To experience the local fare, *Nam Prik Ong* is a must.

Chili Paste
8 whole dried large red chilies, *prik chee fa*, serrano, jalapeño, or California chili
2 tablespoons chopped garlic
3 tablespoons chopped shallot
1 teaspoon shrimp paste

Preparation: Seed and soak the chilies in warm water until soft. Drain and squeeze dry. In a mortar with pestle or food processor, process all ingredients until they form a smooth paste; set aside.

3 tablespoons vegetable oil
1 cup ground lean pork
1 cup chopped cherry tomatoes
2 tablespoons fish sauce, more to taste
1 tablespoon palm sugar, more to taste
2 tablespoons lime juice, more to taste
2 tablespoons chopped cilantro leaf
Fresh vegetables for accompaniment

Preparation: In a pot over medium heat, add the oil and cook the chili paste until fragrant about 3 minutes. Stir in the pork and tomatoes. Break the pork down into smallest chunks and continue cooking until done.

Add the fish sauce, sugar, and lime juice; stir to mix well. Reduce heat to simmer and continue cooking for 7 to 10 minutes.

Transfer into a serving bowl and garnish with the cilantro. Serve the chili dip with fresh vegetables such as cucumber, long beans, carrot, or cabbage.

Northeast
Sap Elee

Arid Land and Creative Eating

The legend *"Gong Kao Noi"* (Small Lunch Box) pertains to the way people in the Northeast eat sticky rice, the staple of local dishes. One day, a short-tempered young farmer left his house to work in the field without having had his breakfast. By late morning, he was getting very hungry and hoped that his frail old mother would deliver his meal sooner than usual. He became greatly irritated and could hardly contain himself when he noticed his mother bringing only a small sphere-shaped lunch box. The old lady protested that she packed the rice tightly and there would be plenty to eat, and she urged him to try it. Consumed with hunger and angry, he struck his mother to death with a plow. He continued to eat his meal, but couldn't even finish half of what was in the lunch box. Finally, he realized the egregious act he had committed and tried to revive his mother, but it was too late. He lived the rest of his life filled with guilt and desperation. To ease the pain, he built a pagoda in the shape of the lunch box, which is called *Gong Kao Noi Pagoda*, to commemorate his mother's death. It exists in *Ubonrajathani* province of the Northeast to this day.

The second largest region in Thailand, the Northeast or *Esan* covers a third of the total land area. "Poor" or "desolate" are words to describe the Northeast, whose population is still predominately small farmers. They depend solely on nature for the right amount of rain to enrich their lands, which contain mostly poor soil. They endure prolonged and frequent droughts or floods. At one time, the drought was so severe that part of the vast barren land was named Kula Rong Hai, which means, "crying Kula." I have been told that *kula* is an indigenous bird, whose habitat often suffers from the drought, but the bird always survives. Once the drought got so intense that even the bird cried. I have also heard that *kula* was a nomadic man capable of surviving many severe living conditions, but he succumbed to crying at this barren area.

The neighboring country, Laos, has long been an influence on the daily life of the Esan people. It shows in the architecture, language,

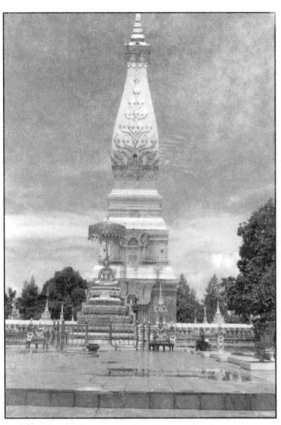

and unique cuisine. Along the Mae Kong River, bordering Thailand and Laos, the *Esan* people speak Laotian fluently, and some have accepted Laotian culture and traditions. In fact, I can't find much difference between *Esan* and Laotian in this part of Thailand except for which side of the Mae Kong River they are from

Facing the extreme conditions, the *Esan* people have had to be resourceful. Their cuisine reflects the creative ways they have of making the best use of local ingredients. Instead of steamed rice, the *Esan* people prefer sticky rice or glutinous rice, which is considered heavier both in weight and how it feels in the stomach. *Laap*, an *Esan* signature dish, employs only a few ingredients, and it is quick and easy to prepare. *Jaew*, or chili dip, is an essential part of the *Esan* meal. The *Esan* people prepare several kinds of fiery hot *Jaew*, to accompany the sticky rice and vegetables during extreme weather conditions. *Esan* soup is also simple to prepare, with one or two dominant flavors

from local herbs and spices, and mostly in clear broth, since they do not have the luxury of coconut milk. Savory *Esan* dishes are usually prepared without sugar. The sweetness comes from creative use of ingredients such as Northeast sweet cilantro, *ngo-gai* or sweet basil, *bai mangluk*.

Whereas natural products from the earth in this region are mostly the same as those in other regions, they are prepared differently. For example, *Tum Som*, the *Esan* green papaya salad, is comprised of papaya, fish sauce, lime juice, and herbs. In contrast, by reversing the name in the Central region to *Som Tum*, elaborate ingredients such as dried or cooked shrimp, tomatoes, sugar, and peanuts are added. *Esan* produces most of Thailand's preserved products, both meats and vegetables, as they never know when the drought or flood will strike. The most famous of these products are raw salt-fermented fish, dried and salt-cured beef, and bamboo shoots in brine. The raw salt-fermented fish appears in several *Esan* dishes as a flavor enhancer. To survive the extreme conditions, the *Esan* people have developed unusual delicacies, such as deep-fried silkworms, grilled lizards, crickets, and red ants salad.

A traditional dinner of the *Esan* called *Pa Khao Lang* is similar to the *Khun Toke* of the North. Guests are offered a tray of local delicacies such as *Laab Moo* (pork salad), bamboo shoot soup, sour fish, salted beef, *Tum Som*, BBQ chicken, *Jaew* dip, vegetables, *Chao Maow* (sweetened puffed rice), and baby bananas. A *katip* (bamboo container) of sticky rice, and water for rinsing hands always accompany the meal.

Anchovy Dip

This chili dip seems to go with everything. It has a permanent place on the dinning table as a condiment. Every Northeastern restaurant prepares the chil dip in big batches and always makes it available to customers. Each restaurant has its own delicious secret recipe for a house chili dip.

2 pieces raw salt-fermented fish or anchovy
2 tablespoons chopped lemongrass, tender part
2 tablespoons chopped shallot
2 tablespoons minced garlic
1 tablespoon chopped galangal
7 whole bird's-eye chilies, more or less to taste
1/4 cup tamarind liquid
1/4 cup fish sauce

Preparation: In a pot, boil 1 cup water with anchovy until the liquid is reduced in half. Roast the lemongrass, shallot, garlic, galangal, and chilies in a pan over a stove or in a 375°F oven until fragrant, about 7 to 10 minutes.

In a mortar with pestle, grind the roasted ingredients until smooth. Stir in the rest of the ingredients to make a chili dip. Or put all ingredients in a food processor and process until well mixed. Transfer to a bowl and serve.

Bamboo Curry

Bamboo grows abundantly in the forest, and its young tender shoots sprout year-round, especially after the rains. Fresh, tender bamboo shoots are not only sweet and crunchy, but also absorb seasonings well, enhancing their neutral, mild taste.

Curry Paste
2 tablespoons chopped garlic
3 tablespoons chopped shallot
1/4 cup sliced large green chili, *prik chee fa,*
    serrano, or jalapeño
2 tablespoons chopped lemongrass, tender part
1 tablespoon chopped galangal

Preparation: In a mortar with pestle or food processor, process all ingredients until they form a smooth paste; set aside.

4 pieces raw salt-fermented fish or anchovy for
    anchovy liquid
1 cup sliced bamboo shoots,
    1/8 inch thick x 1 inch x 2 inches
1 pound catfish fillet or other freshwater fish, sliced
2 tablespoons fish sauce, more to taste
3 tablespoons tamarind liquid, more to taste

Preparation: To make anchovy liquid, boil the raw salt-fermented fish or anchovy with 2 1/2 cups of water. Stir to dilute by breaking them down. Strain to get 2 cups of the thick liquid.

If using fresh bamboo shoots, peel off the tough outer shells. Boil the shoots in several changes of water to get rid of a bitter taste. If using the canned bamboo, boil once to get rid of a preservative taste. Slice or julienne the shoots using only tender parts.

In a pot over medium heat, bring the anchovy liquid to a boil and stir in the chili paste. Add the catfish, bamboo, fish sauce, and tamarind liquid. Stir to mix well and continue cooking until the fish is done, about 3 minutes. Remove from the heat and serve.

Bamboo Shoot Salad

This dish comes with confusion. Its liquid appearance suggests a soup, but its taste and ingredients suggest a salad. And the word Soup in Soup Naw Mai sounds coincidentally like "soup" in English, which adds to even more confusion. In fact, the word soup is a local way of mixing certain ingredients together. Soup or salad, this dish makes the best use of bamboo in both flavor and texture, and it is a popular dish.

> 2 cups shredded bamboo shoots
> 3 pieces raw salt-fermented fish or anchovy
> 1 bunch *Bai Yanang* (or 1 cup canned liquid)
> 1 tablespoon rice grains
> 2 teaspoons ground chili, more or less to taste
> 3 tablespoons fish sauce, more to taste
> 3 tablespoons lime juice, more to taste
> 1/4 cup chopped lemon basil leaves, *bai mangluk*
> 1/4 cup chopped mint leaves
> 6 whole long beans for accompaniment
> 1 head cabbage or lettuce for accompaniment

Preparation: If using fresh bamboo shoots, peel off the tough outer shells and boil with several changes of water to get rid off a bitter taste. For canned shoots, boil once to get rid of a preservative flavor. Shred the shoots into long, thin strips and squeeze out the liquid.

To make the anchovy liquid, in a pot, combine 3 pieces of raw salt-fermented fish or anchovy with 3/4 cup of water. Bring the mixture to a boil and break down the anchovy to dilute with water. Strain the mixture to get 3 tablespoons of the thick liquid.

To make *Bai Yanang* liquid, process the *Bai Yanang* leaves in a mortar with pestle or in a food processor until smooth. In a pot, combine the leaves with 1 cup of water and bring it to a boil. Strain the mixture to get 1 cup of the thick liquid.

oast the rice grains in a pan over a stove until light brown and fragrant. Let
ool and grind in a mortar or food processor until coarsely ground.

a bowl, combine the bamboo, anchovy liquid, *Bai Yanang* liquid, roasted
ce, ground chili, fish sauce, and lime juice. Stir and fold to mix thoroughly.
djust the taste with more fish sauce and lime juice. Garnish with the basil
d mint leaves before serving with the accompaniments.

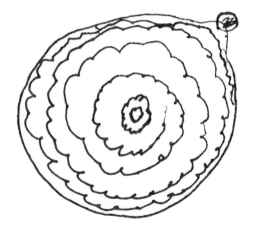

Barbequed Chicken, Northeast

The Northeast version of this dish is simple in both ingredients and cookir
preparation. It has gained popularity throughout Thailand as a dish that goes
well with Green Papaya Salad (page 78 and 123) and sticky rice. The recipe
calls for home-raised chicken or spring chicken, whose meat has less fat, a
denser texture, and better taste than farm-raised chicken. Grilling or broiling
over hot coals enhances the smoky aroma of the roasted garlic flavor.

> 1 whole spring chicken (about 2 pounds)
> 1 teaspoon salt
> 3 tablespoons minced garlic
> 1 teaspoon ground white pepper
> 3 tablespoons minced cilantro roots or stems (optional)
> 1/4 cup minced lemongrass, tender part (optional)

Preparation: Clean the chicken and split it in half lengthwise or cut into
body parts.

In a mortar with pestle or food processor, process the salt, garlic, and pepper
(and cilantro and lemongrass, if using) until they form a smooth paste. Rub
the mixture all over the chicken and marinate overnight or at least 2 hours in
refrigerator.

Prepare firewood or char-
coal 30 minutes in advance,
so that the coals reach a
stage of medium heat.
Barbecue the chicken for 15
minutes on each side or
until the chicken is golden
brown and cooked through.

Serve the dish with
Anchovy Dip (page 66) or
Thai Sweet Chili Sauce (see
glossary) and sticky rice.

Beef Stew

This smoldering hot clear soup is considered a comfort food of the Northeast. Any part of beef including the intestine, liver, and lung are slow-cooked until tender, and will melt in your mouth. The soup can be served as a mellow broth without lime juice or chili, or as a pungent, hot and sour soup with all the attendant herbs and spices.

>2 pounds beef fillet, top or bottom round
>6 pieces thinly sliced galangal
>3 stalks lemongrass, cut into
>   2-inch-long pieces and bruised
>5 whole kaffir lime leaves
>2 tablespoons rice grains
>1/4 cup fish sauce or anchovy liquid, more to taste
>1 tablespoon beef bouillon
>2 tablespoons thinly sliced shallot
>2 tablespoons chili flakes (optional)
>1/4 cup lime juice, more to taste
>1 cup sweet basil leaves, *bai horapha*
>2 cups chopped morning glory or cabbage
>1/4 cup chopped cilantro and
>   green onion mix for garnish

Preparation: Dice the beef into bite-size pieces. In a pot over medium-low heat, combine the beef, 6 cups water, galangal, lemongrass, and kaffir lime. Slow cook the mixture until the beef is tender, 20 to 30 minutes.

Roast the rice in a pan over a stove until light brown and fragrant. Let cool and process in a mortar or food processor until roughly ground.

Bring the soup to a boil and stir in the fish sauce and beef bouillon. Remove from the heat and then add the shallot, roasted rice, chili flakes, and lime juice. Adjust the taste with more fish sauce and lime juice.

To serve, line a serving bowl with the sweet basil and morning glory. Pour the smoldering soup over the vegetables and garnish with the cilantro and green onion.

Grilled Beef Salad

This dish provides a full-tasting impact for those who enjoy good quality beef. The acidity of the lime cures the beef just right for the combination of flavors and refreshing taste. The dish must be eaten immediately after preparation.

1 tablespoon rice grains
1 pound beef tenderloin
1/4 cup fish sauce, more to taste
1/4 cup lime juice, more to taste
1 tablespoon granulated sugar (optional)
1 tablespoon very thinly sliced lemongrass, tender part
1/4 cup thinly sliced shallot or red onion
1 cup thinly sliced English cucumber (optional)
1/2 cup seeded julienned tomatoes (optional)
1 teaspoon chopped bird's-eye chilies,
    more or less to taste
2 tablespoons chopped cilantro leaves
2 tablespoons chopped green onion
2 tablespoons chopped mint leaves
1 head lettuce or cabbage for accompaniment

Preparation: Roast the rice in a pan over a stove until light brown and fragrant. Let cool and grind in a mortar or food processor until roughly ground.

Cook the beef by grilling, sautéing, or roasting until medium-rare or at your desire doneness. Slice the beef thinly across the grain.

In a bowl, combine the fish sauce, lime juice, and sugar if using, to make a dressing.

To serve, combine the beef with all ingredients *except* dressing and lettuce and toss with the dressing, little dressing at a time then taste. Serve with fresh vegetables such as lettuce, cabbage, and long beans for accompaniments.

Grilled Pork Neck

Serves 4

Pork neck provides a unique texture with the right combination of meat, muscle, and fat. It is also priced dearly because of its flavor, which some describe as nutty sweet. To achieve the best taste, the pork should be marinated and then grilled over an open flame to get a hint of smokiness. It is usually served with a dipping sauce and accompaniments such as sliced fresh ginger, cucumber, and roasted peanuts.

> 1 pound pork neck
> 2 tablespoons chopped garlic
> 3 tablespoons chopped cilantro root or stem
> 1 teaspoon ground white pepper
> 1/2 teaspoon salt
> 2 tablespoons granulated sugar (optional)
> 2 tablespoons fish sauce
> 2 tablespoons Maggi seasoning

Preparation: Rinse the pork with water and slice into 2-inch-thick, long strips. Set aside to drain.

In a mortar with pestle or food processor, process the garlic, cilantro root, pepper, salt, and sugar if using until they form a smooth paste.

In a bowl, combine the pork, paste, fish sauce, and Maggi seasoning. Mix thoroughly and marinate for at least 30 minutes.

Prepare a firewood or charcoal grill 30 minutes in advance to get medium heat. Grill the pork 7 to 10 minutes on each side until done.

Slice the pork across the grain into thin pieces and serve with the chili dipping sauce (page 66).

Ground Beef Salad

Laab is the local word for preparing a refreshing salad by a quick blending of ground meat, fresh herbs, and lime juice. Most Northerners prefer the beef raw, letting the acidic lime juice cure the meat during the mixing process. *Laab Muu* (pork), *Laab Kai* (chicken), or *Laab Ped* (duck) can be substituted for the *Laab Nuea* (beef). This salad is traditionally eaten with sticky rice. An array of fresh vegetables, such as lettuce, cabbage, and long beans are essential accompaniments.

1 thin slice galangal
2 tablespoons rice grains
1 pound ground or minced beef
1/2 cup thinly sliced shallot or red onion
1/4 cup lime juice, more to taste
1/4 cup fish sauce, more to taste
1 tablespoon granulated sugar (optional)
2 tablespoons chopped cilantro leaves
2 tablespoons chopped green onion
1 tablespoon chopped mint leaves
1 teaspoon chili flakes, more or less to taste
1 head lettuce or cabbage for accompaniment

Preparation: Roast the galangal and the rice in a pan over a stove or in a 375°F oven until light brown and fragrant, about 7 to 10 minutes. Let cool and grind in a mortar or food processor until roughly ground.

In a pot over medium heat, cook the beef with 1/4 cup water until done to taste. Break the beef down into smallest chunks.

Remove from the heat and stir in the galangal-rice powder, shallot, lime juice, and fish sauce. Mix thoroughly and then add the cilantro, green onion, mint, and chili flakes.

Season to taste with more lime juice and fish sauce. Serve with fresh vegetables, such as lettuce, cabbage, and long beans.

This is another version of *Laab*, a Northeast salad that is packed with flavor. Using fresh fish fillet, this version has less fat and calls for a special type of cilantro to tame the fishy taste. A combination of fresh lime juice, shallot, and mint leaves gives it a refreshing taste.

1/2 pound fish fillet of choice
2 tablespoons rice grains
1 thin slice galangal
3 tablespoons shredded Northeast sweet cilantro, *ngo-gai*
2 tablespoons chili flakes, more or less to taste
3 tablespoons thinly sliced shallot
2 tablespoons chopped green onion
1/4 cup fish sauce, more to taste
1/4 cup lime juice, more to taste
1 tablespoon granulated sugar (optional)
1 tablespoon chopped mint leaves
1 head cabbage or lettuce for accompaniment
6 whole long beans for accompaniment

Preparation: Poach the fish in boiling water or steam until done. Break the fish into small chunks.

Roast the rice with the galangal in a pan over a stove or in a 375°F oven until they are light brown and fragrant, about 7 to 10 minutes. Let cool and grind in a mortar or food processor until roughly ground.

Stack and roll 3 to 4 Northeast cilantro leaves tightly into a cigarette-like roll. Slice very thin and unravel into fine strips.

In a bowl, combine the fish, chili flakes, ground rice-galangal, shallot, cilantro, and green onion. Add the fish sauce, lime juice, sugar if using, and mint. Stir and mix thoroughly. Adjust the taste with more fish sauce and lime juice.

Serve the fish salad with the vegetable accompaniments on the side.

Liver Salad

Tub Wa

Serves

This dish offers a distinct, sweet flavor of beef liver. The less the liver is cooked, the sweeter it becomes. It's quite a popular delicacy in the Northeast where food is sometimes not so abundant and so all animal parts are used. In the United States, the cattle industry uses high standards and produces high-quality sanitized beef products. Taking precautions and cooking the liver completely will assure you of the meat's safety.

> 1 pound beef liver
> 2 tablespoons rice grains
> 1/4 cup lime juice, more to taste
> 2 tablespoons thinly sliced shallot
> 1/4 cup fish sauce, more to taste
> 1 tablespoon chili flakes, more or less to taste
> 1 tablespoon chopped mint leaves
> 1 bunch lemon basil, *bai mangluk*, for accompaniment
> 1 head cabbage or lettuce for accompaniment
> 6 whole long beans for accompaniment

Preparation: Rinse the liver with water and slice into 1/4-inch thick x 1/2-inch x 2-inch strips. Poach the liver in boiling water to desired doneness. Strain and let dry.

Roast the rice in a pan over a stove until light brown and fragrant. Let cool and grind coarsely in a mortar or food processor.

In a bowl, combine the liver with lime juice and mix thoroughly. Add the roasted rice, shallot, fish sauce, chili flakes, and mint leaves. Mix well and adjust the taste with more lime juice and fish sauce.

Serve the liver with the accompaniments.

Mushroom Soup

After the rains, mushrooms spring up almost everywhere in Thailand. Freshly picked mushrooms are superb for this smoldering, hot and spicy, clear soup. The recipe is simple and quick to prepare and converts easily into a vegetarian dish. Lemon basil, *Bai Mangluk*, which provides a sweet, lemony flavor, makes the dish unique.

> 3 vegetable bouillon cubes or 3 cups vegetable stock
> 4 cups oyster mushrooms (or other mushrooms)
> 1/4 cup chopped dried red chili, more or less to taste
> 2 tablespoons chopped lemongrass, tender part
> 1/2 teaspoon salt
> 3 pieces raw salt-fermented fish or anchovy (optional)
> 2 tablespoons fish sauce
> 1/2 cup lemon basil leaves, *bai mangluk*

Preparation: To make the vegetable stock, combine 3 tablespoons of vegetable bouillon with 3 cups of water. (Or use ready-made stock.)

Shred the oyster mushroom into bite-size pieces.

In a mortar with pestle or food processor, process the chili, lemongrass, and salt until well mixed.

To make the anchovy liquid, combine 3 pieces of raw salt-fermented fish or anchovy with 1 cup of water in a pot and bring it to a boil. Stir and break the anchovy down to dilute and then strain to get 1/4 cup thick liquid.

In a pot over medium heat, combine the vegetable stock, chili mixture, and anchovy liquid. Bring it to a boil and add the mushrooms and fish sauce. Continue cooking until the mushrooms are done and then add the lemon basil. Remove from the heat and serve.

Papaya Salad, Northeast

This is another variety of salad, whose simplicity brings out the best. This dish uses a few simple ingredients to produce a great impact. It has few calories and no fat, yet is filled with fiber and minerals. In addition to the papaya, the locals also prepare it with cucumber, long beans, carrots, or unripe bananas. The salad is a popular component of lunch fare: barbecued chicken, papaya salad, and sticky rice.

> 1 green papaya (2 pounds)
> 2 pieces raw salt-fermented fish or anchovy
> 5 whole fresh bird's-eye chilies, more or less to taste
> 2 tablespoons chopped garlic
> 8 whole cherry tomatoes, cut in half
> 1/4 cup long beans, cut 1-inch long
> 3 tablespoons lime juice, more to taste
> 2 tablespoons fish sauce, more to taste
> 1 head cabbage or lettuce for accompaniment
> 8 whole long beans for accompaniment

Preparation: Peel and seed the green papaya. Rinse with cold water and shred into fine strains with a shredder or knife, to make 3 cups.

To make the anchovy liquid, boil 1/2 cup of water with the raw salt-fermented fish or anchovy and break them down to dilute. Strain and reserve 2 tablespoons of the liquid.

In a clay mortar with a wooden pestle or an aluminum bowl with a rolling pin, smash the chilies and garlic until well mixed. Add the papaya, tomatoes, and long beans. Continue working the pestle to mix well.

Add the anchovy liquid, lime juice, and fish sauce. Continue smashing and folding until all ingredients are thoroughly combined and the papaya absorbs all flavors.

Adjust the taste with more lime juice and fish sauce. Serve the salad with the accompaniments.

Phla is a word describing a fresh, quickly prepared lime-cured dish. The original recipe calls for uncooked prawns. Other meats can also be used depending on your taste. The ingredients of shredded kaffir lime leaf and lemongrass make the dish unique. Sharp, refreshing lime should enhance the flavor of the dish, bringing out a hint of fish.

> 1 pound prawns, shelled and deveined
> 5 whole bird's-eye chilies, more or less to taste
> 1 stalk lemongrass, tender part, finely shredded
> 2 to 3 kaffir lime leaves
> 2 tablespoons thinly sliced shallot or red onion
> 3 tablespoons lime juice, more to taste
> 3 tablespoons fish sauce, more to taste
> 3 sprigs mint leaves
> 1 head lettuce or cabbage for accompaniment

Preparation: Poach the prawns in boiling water until almost done, 2 to 3 minutes.

For a mild chili flavor, smash the bird's-eye chilies lightly and leave them whole, otherwise chop or mince the chilies fine.

Peel tough outer shells off the lemongrass. Slice the tender, inner portions into thin, very fine rings. Stack couple kaffir lime leaves and roll tightly. Slice the roll thinly and unravel into fine strips.

In a bowl, combine the prawn with the lime juice and fish sauce. Add the chilies, lemongrass, shallot, and kaffir lime; toss to mix well. Adjust the taste with more lime juice and fish sauce.

Transfer to a serving platter and garnish with the mint leaves. Serve with the accompaniments.

Steamed Whole Fish   *Nueng Pla*

Serves 6

Steaming is the simplest cooking method and allows ingredients to maintain their fullest flavors. Several varieties of fresh-caught freshwater fish, such as bass, tilapia, and snakehead, yield the sweetest flavors. The Northerner usually dips a ball of sticky rice into the liquid of the steamed fish and enjoys the delicious combination of sweet and sour.

- 1 whole 2-pound fish, scaled and gutted
- 1/2 teaspoon salt
- 1/4 teaspoon ground pepper
- 6 pieces very thinly sliced galangal
- 6 whole kaffir lime leaves
- 2 stalks lemongrass, cut into 2-inch long pieces and bruised
- 2 tablespoons thinly sliced garlic
- 3 tablespoons thinly sliced shallot
- 6 whole bird's-eye chilies, bruised
- 1/4 cup fish sauce, more to taste
- 1/4 cup tamarind liquid
- 2 tablespoons lime juice, more to taste
- 3 tablespoons chopped cilantro and green onion for garnish

Preparation: Cut 5 deep slashes on each side of the fish. Rub the fish with the salt and pepper thoroughly.

In a large plate deep enough to hold the liquid from steaming, place half of the galangal, kaffir lime, and lemongrass on the bottom. Place the whole fish over the herbs and then place the remaining herbs on top of the fish.

In a bowl, combine the garlic, shallot, chilies, fish sauce, tamarind liquid, and lime juice. Sprinkle the mixture all over the fish.

Place the plate of fish in a steamer over high heat and steam for 20 minutes until the fish is done. A wok with lid can also be used as a steamer.

Taste the liquid in the bottom of the plate and adjust the taste with more fish sauce and lime juice. Garnish with the cilantro and green onion before serving.

80   The Best of Regional Thai Cuisine

Sun-dried Beef

This dish reminds me of beef jerky, a popular snack in the United States. In the Northeast, sun-dried beef is also popular as a snack and can be served as a main dish with sticky rice. Only one day of sunshine is required in the sun-dry process to ensure the right texture of beef. To cook the beef, simply fry it in hot oil until done or fry it longer for an extra crispy texture.

> 2 pounds beef fillet, top or bottom round
> 2 teaspoons salt
> 1 tablespoon ground coriander
> 1 tablespoon ground black pepper
> 1 cup vegetable oil for frying

Preparation: Slice the beef across the grain into very thin, long strips.

Combine the salt, coriander, and pepper; sprinkle all over the beef. Mix thoroughly and set aside to marinate for at least 30 minutes.

Separate the beef strips and arrange tightly but not overlapping on a tray with wax paper. Place the tray in a sunny spot unreachable by pets or scavengers. Or hang the beef strips on a string in a sunny spot. Dry the beef for a day or at least 6 hours until it is semidried.

In a pan over medium heat, add the oil and fry the beef until done, 5 to 7 minutes. Or fry longer for extra crispy. Remove from the oil and drain over absorbent papers. Serve the beef as a beef jerky snack or with sticky rice as a meal.

Central
Aroi Maak

Fertile Basin and Capital City

A little-known legend of the Central region is the story of *Nak Prakanong*. Her ghostly demeanor has been told throughout the generations, in Thai TV series and in movies, and has terrified viewers the way Linda Blair did in *The Exorcist*.

Nak was an ordinary woman whose talent lay in concocting superb chili dips with a mortar and pestle. The dips seduced one young man into love and finally marriage. The couple lived happily and expected a child. In the sixth month of pregnancy, the husband was recruited to fight in a war, leaving Nak on her own among distant neighbors. She delivered, with severe complications. Though help came from a midwife and neighbors, unfortunately Nak did not survive and the baby was stillborn. This kind of death was believed, among Thais, to manifest the most powerful and haunting ghost of all, as it possessed combined powers of both mother and child. News of the tragic death troubled the villagers, and her ghostly appearance horrified them. The sound of a baby's lullaby could be heard from the woman's empty hut, and sometimes the image of a woman carrying a child had been witnessed. The husband finally returned from the war. The villagers warned him of the family demise, but he wanted to see for himself. He came to the hut and found Nak still crying over the loss of her child. He assumed that the villagers had misinformed him about a double death.

The couple resumed an ostensibly normal life of husband and wife, he suspecting nothing. Nak played the role of Thai wife, cooking and cleaning for her husband. She concealed her ghostly powers from her husband. But once, she slipped. One day while she was using a mortar and pestle to make a chili dip, she accidentally dropped the pestle through a hole in the kitchen floor. Instead of walking downstairs, as the hut was on stilts, she extended her arm through the hole to pick up the pestle. This phenomenon shook her husband so profoundly that he ran away. Nak became so agitated that she scared the entire village out of their wits. No one left the house after nightfall. Experts had been employed to perform exorcism to get rid of Nak, but all of them succumbed to her power, and some were even killed. Finally, a respected monk successfully trapped her spirit in a clay pot and sealed and stashed it in an undisclosed location. To this

day, local people are still afraid that someday the pot will be discovered and broken, freeing the spirit for another haunting.

The Central region has fertile flatlands which spread out around the Choa Praya River, the lifeblood of the region. The river originates in northern waterways, which carry silt and nutrition and revitalize the Central land annually. The land yields large-quantity, high-quality agricultural products all year-round with the support of a complex irrigation network. This network also serves as a commuter highway for people and goods, and the region is dubbed the "Venice of the East." Bangkok, the capital city, is the center of Thai economy, politics, and culture. It houses all major government institutions, including the leading educational, medical, sporting, and cultural facilities. The capital city is centrally located and flanked by the gulf of Thailand where sea-going ships traverse. Bangkok attracts people from all regions, mostly for economic reasons, and its population exceeds 10 million. Similar to any big city, Bangkok has become a metropolis with its own set of problems. The high price of being a capital city is that it is one of the world's most polluted and congested cities. Each year, due to inadequate drainage, flooding periodically paralyzes the city and hardened the life of its inhabitants. Despite these obstacles, Bangkok still grows and attracts more people, yielding a colorful conglomeration of flavors and cuisines.

The best food merchants bring their trade to Bangkok to challenge an elaborate, sophisticated and contemporary food scene. The Central region covers both sides of the Gulf of Thailand where abundant supplies of seafood

The Best of Regional Thai Cuisine

are transported daily for enormous consumption in Bangkok. Along the Gulf, cities such as Rayong, produce one of the best *nam pla*, fish sauce and *kapi*, shrimp paste, which are essential to almost all Thai dishes. All year-round, the Central plain produces the majority of the country's fruits and vegetables, such as *som keow wan*, sweet tangerine and *mamoung*, mango. These fruits and vegetables, along with seasonal fruits and vegetables imported from other regions, make Bangkok markets perpetually vibrant with colors and choices.

Food of the Central region, especially in Bangkok, has often been modified

to fit ever-changing trends. It frequently reinvents itself to keep up with the demands of challenging new tastes, utilizing the influx of new ingredients, and accommodating new life styles. Every visit to Thailand during the past years, I've found and tasted creative concoctions mixing and matching local ingredients and techniques in new dishes. At this point, I have to credit this new generation of chefs who break through a traditional and conservative barrier in Thai cooking and bring its cuisine to new heights.

Barbecued Chicken, Central   *Gai Yang Kati*

The many versions of this dish suggest steep competition among regions. You need to try them all to find your favorite recipe. This recipe uses many elaborate ingredients, especially herbs and spices. It uses coconut in a marinade to make the chicken creamier, nuttier, and sweeter, and yields a moist and tender texture after being barbecued over an open flame.

> 2 tablespoons finely minced garlic
> 1 tablespoon finely minced cilantro roots or stems
> 1 tablespoon finely minced ginger
> 2 tablespoons finely minced lemongrass, tender part
> 1 teaspoon ground white pepper
> 2 tablespoons cognac or cooking wine
> 2 tablespoons fish sauce
> 2 tablespoons Maggi seasoning
> 1/2 teaspoon salt
> 1 tablespoon granulated sugar
> 1/4 cup coconut cream
> 2 pounds chicken legs and thighs

Preparation: Process the garlic, cilantro, ginger, lemongrass, and white pepper in a mortar with pestle or a food processor until well mixed. Combine with the rest of the ingredients and stir until the sugar is dissolved. Marinate the chicken overnight or at least 2 hours.

Prepare the firewood or charcoal 30 minutes ahead of time and grill the chicken over medium heat until done, 7 to 10 minutes on each side.

Serve the chicken with the Thai sweet chili sauce, *Nam Jim Gai* (see glossary).

Catfish Puff Salad

Yum Pladuk Foo

Serves 6

This is an innovative way to transform a simple fish salad into an exciting feast, combining the crunchy textures of fried fish and fresh fruits with the sharp tastes of lime juice and palm sugar dressing. It should be eaten immediately after all ingredients have been tossed to ensure the freshest impact. Chill the fruits, vegetables and dressing before mixing to get a cold, crisp, and clean explosion in your mouth.

> 2 pieces catfish fillet or a whole fish
> 3 cups vegetable oil for deep-frying
> 2 whole eggs, beaten (optional)
> 1/2 cup cornstarch or tempura batter mix
> 1 cup finely shredded green unripe mango
> 1 cup finely shredded Granny Smith apple
> 1/2 cup thinly sliced red onion or shallot
> 2 cups shredded lettuce
> 1/4 cup chopped roasted peanuts for garnish
> 2 tablespoons chopped cilantro leaves for garnish

Preparation: Grill the fish on an open flame or bake in a 350°F oven until done, about 7 to 10 minutes. Shred the meat with a fork so its surface is rough and puffy or break the meat into small chunks and form small patties.

In a pan over medium heat, add the oil and heat to 350° to 375°F. Dip the fish in the beaten egg and roll in the cornstarch. Deep-fry in the hot oil until puffed and golden brown; set aside.

Dressing
1/4 cup fish sauce
1/4 cup lime juice
3 tablespoons palm or granulated sugar
1 tablespoon bird's-eye chilies, more or less to taste

Preparation: Combine all ingredients for the dressing and stir until the sugar is dissolved.

–continued–

To serve, combine the catfish, mango, apple, and onion. Toss with the dressing, a little dressing at a time and taste.

Arrange the lettuce on a serving platter and top with the catfish mixture. Garnish with the chopped nuts and cilantro.

It can also be served in layers of ingredient with the puffed catfish on top and the dressing on the side. The salad can be spooned in a small amount at a time and top with the dressing individually.

Cauliflower Sour Curry

Gaeng Som Goong Galum

This dish is a curry soup made of light spicy broth and sweet and sour tamarind liquid, without any coconut product. It is a refreshing change from the rich, creamy, heavily coconut-based curries. If you don't like cauliflower, napa cabbage, long beans, or swamp cabbage can be delicious substitutes.

> 1 pound shrimp or prawns, peeled and deveined
> 2 tablespoons shrimp bouillon (optional)
> 1/8 cup dried shrimp, soaked in warm water
> 1/4 cup Gaeng Som Curry Paste (page 33)
> 2 cups cauliflower florets
> 3 tablespoons fish sauce, more to taste
> 1/4 cup tamarind liquid, more to taste
> 1 tablespoon granulated sugar (optional)

Preparation: Peel and clean the fresh shrimp or prawns and save the shells for stock. Boil the shells with 3 cups of water for 10 minutes and strain to get 2 cups stock. Or dilute the shrimp bouillon with 2 cups of water to make the stock.

Soak the dried shrimp in warm water until soft. Drain and grind in a mortar with pestle or food processor until they form a smooth paste.

In a pot over medium heat, add the stock and stir in the curry paste and dried shrimp paste. Bring the stock to a boil and add the fresh shrimp or prawns, cauliflower, fish sauce, tamarind liquid, and sugar; mix well. Continue cooking until the shrimp and cauliflower are done, 5 to 7 minutes.

Adjust the taste with more fish sauce and tamarind liquid. Serve with steamed rice.

Not only do Thais borrow a variety of spices from the Spice Islands but they also adopt the popular dish, satay—food on skewers—from Indonesia. To make the satay more original, Thais add local herbs and spices and serve the satay with the Thai version of peanut sauce.

3 cups (2 pounds) chicken tenders or meat
2 tablespoons chopped shallot
1 tablespoon chopped garlic
1 tablespoon chopped galangal
1 tablespoon chopped lemongrass, tender part
1 tablespoon ground turmeric
1 teaspoon salt
3 tablespoons granulated sugar
1/4 cup vegetable oil
1/4 cup coconut cream
1 package bamboo skewers, soaked in cold water

Preparation: Cut the chicken into long, thin strips.

In a mortar with pestle or food processor, process the shallot, garlic, galangal, and lemongrass until they form a smooth paste.

In a bowl, combine the chicken, paste, turmeric, salt, sugar, and oil. Marinate the chicken overnight or at least 2 hours before skewering with the bamboo sticks. Soaking the bamboo sticks in water before skewering helps prevent them from burning.

Prepare a firewood or charcoal grill 30 minutes ahead of time and grill the chicken over medium heat, brushing with the coconut cream and turning occasionally until the chicken is done, 5 to 7 minutes on each side.

Serve the satay with Peanut Sauce (page 124) and Cucumber Salad, *Ajad* (page 98) as an accompaniment.

Sweet crunchiness makes this dish highly appealing. In the United States, sweet corn in season makes the best staple for this simple dish. The best corn, combined with exotic ingredients, is the recipe for delicious success.

2 cups sweet corn kernels,
  fresh cut from the cob (3 ears)
1 whole egg
1 teaspoon salt
2 teaspoons very finely minced garlic
1/4 teaspoon ground white pepper
1/4 cup all-purpose flour
3 tablespoons coconut milk, more or less for texture
2 cups vegetable oil for deep-frying

Preparation: Combine all ingredients *except* the oil. Knead until they form stiff dough. Add more coconut milk as needed.

Heat the oil in a pan to 350° to 375°F, form about 1 tablespoon of the corn mixture into a thin patty and fry in the hot oil until golden brown on both sides. Remove from the oil and drain over absorbent papers.

Serve the patties with dipping sauce.

Dipping Sauce
1/4 cup distilled vinegar
1 tablespoon granulated sugar
1 teaspoon salt
1 teaspoon minced red chili, more or less to taste
1/2 cup thinly sliced cucumber (optional)
1/4 cup chopped roasted peanuts

Preparation: Combine the vinegar, sugar, and salt in a small pot and bring to a boil. Cook until the sugar is dissolved and the mixture turns syrupy. Remove from the heat and let cool before adding the rest of the ingredients.

Crab in Coconut Curry

Both crab and fish are combined in this recipe. The original recipe calls for fish, but in the innovative creative Central region, crab or other shellfish have been added to enhance the dish. The dish is usually prepared in individual portions, each one large enough to serve one person. Small bowls made of banana leaf lend authentic appeal, and even small crab shells provide an unusual touch.

Chili Paste
10 whole dried large red chilies, *prik chee fa*, serrano, jalapeño, or California chili
1/2 teaspoon salt
1/2 teaspoon chopped galangal
2 tablespoons chopped lemongrass, tender part
1 teaspoon shredded kaffir lime skin or leaf
1 teaspoon shredded lesser ginger, *krachai* (optional)
1 teaspoon chopped garlic
1 teaspoon chopped shallot
1 teaspoon whole black pepper
1 teaspoon chopped cilantro root or stem
1 teaspoon shrimp paste

Preparation: Seed and soak the dried chili in warm water until soft. Drain and squeeze dry. In a mortar with pestle or food processor, process all ingredients until they form a smooth paste.

1 fresh white fish fillet, about 1/2 pound
2 tablespoons fish sauce
2 cups coconut cream
1/2 cup sliced Inoki mushrooms or napa cabbage,
   1-inch long
1 cup crabmeat
1 whole egg
1 tablespoon crumbled shrimp bouillon
1 tablespoon very finely shredded kaffir lime leaf
4 pieces crab shell, medium-size or
   1 large banana leaf (optional)
2 teaspoons rice flour or cornstarch
3 sprigs cilantro leaf for garnish
1 tablespoon very finely shredded red chili or bell pepper

Preparation: Chop the fish into small chunks. In a bowl, combine the fish, fish sauce, and chili paste.

Stir in 1 cup of coconut cream in 1/4 cup increments, and stir vigorously and constantly until well mixed.

Add the mushrooms, crabmeat, egg, shrimp bouillon, and shredded kaffir lime. Stir to mix well.

To make banana bowls, cut the banana leaf into 8 round pieces, each with a 7-inch diameter. For each bowl, stack 2 pieces to double the thickness and fold the edges, forming 4 corners in a bowl, and hold in shape with toothpicks or staples.

Fill the crab shells, banana bowls, or small ramekins high with the crab mixture.

In a pot over medium heat, combine the remaining 1 cup coconut cream with flour. Cook and stir until thick. Spread about 1 tablespoon of the mixture over the crab and garnish with the cilantro leaf and shredded red chili.

In a steamer over high heat, steam the stuffed crab for 15 to 20 minutes until done. Serve the crab with steamed jasmine rice.

Crepe (Yuan)

The name of this dish *"Yuan"* suggests Vietnamese origin, whose comparable dish can be found in high-end Vietnamese restaurants. Thais have adapted the dish, modified the taste, and added ingredients such as shredded coconut to call it their own. The dish requires many steps of preparation and many elaborate ingredients that were originally fit for the royal court. You can also find this dish at a specialized hawker's stand. Special occasions call for a special feast and *Kanom Bueng Yuan* is a worthy contender.

Batter
3/4 cup rice flour
2 tablespoons all-purpose flour
1 teaspoon baking soda
1 cups coconut milk
1 whole egg
1 tablespoon granulated sugar
1 teaspoon ground turmeric
1/2 teaspoon salt
1/8 cup vegetable oil

Preparation: Combine all ingredients and gently beat until smooth. Set aside for at least 30 minutes. Before using, add more coconut milk or water if the batter is too thick.

Filling
1/2 cup shredded coconut or coconut flakes
2 tablespoons vegetable oil
2 tablespoons finely minced garlic
2 tablespoons finely minced shallot
1 cup shrimp, peeled and deveined
1/8 cup dried shrimp (optional)
1 cup thinly sliced fried tofu
1 cup thinly sliced shiitake mushrooms
   (or other mushrooms)
2 tablespoons fish sauce
1/2 teaspoon ground pepper
2 tablespoons granulated sugar
1/4 cup finely minced preserved turnip
1/4 cup chopped roasted peanuts

1 1/2 cups bean sprouts
1/2 cup chopped cilantro leaf for garnish
1/2 cup shredded colored bell pepper for garnish

Preparation: Roast the shredded coconut or coconut flakes in a 350°F oven or dry roast in a pan over a stove until light brown and fragrant, about 5 to 7 minutes.

Heat a pan over medium heat, add the oil, and cook the garlic and shallot until fragrant. Add both types of shrimp, tofu, and mushrooms and cook until the shrimp are done. Then add the fish sauce, ground pepper, sugar, turnip, peanuts, and coconut flakes. Stir to mix well and set aside. Add some water if the mixture is too dry.

In a 10-inch nonstick pan over medium heat, brush just enough oil to coat the pan. Pour 1/2 cup of the batter in the pan and swirl the batter to thinly coat the pan's surface. Cook the batter for 2 to 5 minutes until firm; do not attempt to turn over the crepe.

Add about 3/4 cup of the filling, spreading over one half of the crepe. Top the filling with the bean sprouts and cilantro. Fold the other half of the crepe to cover the filling.

To remove the crepe from the pan, invert a serving plate and cover the top of the pan. Place your hand over the plate and turn over the pan to flip the crepe onto the plate.

Garnish the crepe with more cilantro and colored pepper and serve with the Cucumber Salad, *Ajad* (page 98).

Crispy Noodles

My mother was well known for her *Mee Grop*, whose noodles stayed crispy longer than anybody else's. Unfortunately, her secret recipe died with her and I still cannot replicate her specialty. This dish requires many steps and ingredients to prepare. The noodles are fried until crispy and puffed light with air and then tossed with a sweet and sour sauce. It is great as an appetizer and you won't be able to stop after the first bite.

Noodles
6 ounces dried vermicelli rice noodles, *Sen Mee*
3 cups vegetable oil for deep-frying

Preparation: Heat the oil in a large pan or wok to 375° to 400°F; deep-fry the noodles, a little portion at a time and turning, until fully puffed. Set aside.

Sauce
1 tablespoon vegetable oil
2 tablespoons minced shallot
2 tablespoons minced garlic
1/2 cup tamarind liquid or distilled vinegar
1/2 cup palm sugar
2 tablespoons lime juice
1/4 cup fish sauce
2 tablespoons tomato paste for red color (optional)

Preparation: In a pot over medium heat, add the oil and cook the shallot and garlic until fragrant. Add the rest of the ingredients and cook the mixture until it turns syrupy, about 10 to 15 minutes.

Garnish
2 tablespoons vegetable oil
3 tablespoons very thinly sliced shallot
1/2 cup dried shrimp
2 whole eggs, beaten
1 cup fresh shrimp, peeled and deveined
1 cup thinly sliced tofu, fried
1/8 cup garlic chives, 1-inch long
1/4 cup thinly sliced red bell pepper
1 tablespoon thinly sliced pickled garlic

2 tablespoons orange zest for garnish (optional)
2 tablespoons chopped cilantro leaf
2 cups bean sprouts

Preparation: Heat the oil in a saucepan and fry the shallot until light brown and crispy. Set aside. In the same pan, fry the dried shrimp until light brown and crispy. Set aside.

In the same pan with a thin coat of oil, add the eggs and swirl to thinly coat the pan's surface. Cook the omelet until done and slice into long, thin strips; set aside.

In the same pan, add the fresh shrimp and cook until done with a little sauce; set aside.

To serve, in a large-size bowl, combine the noodles, shrimp, and tofu. Toss in the sauce, a little at a time and taste the mixture. Add the chives, red bell pepper, and pickled garlic; combine well.

Transfer to a serving platter, top with the omelet, fried shallot, fried shrimp, orange zest, and chopped cilantro. Serve the crispy noodles with the fresh bean sprouts.

Ajad plays many roles in Thai meals. It is served as a sauce for crepes, fish cakes, and shrimp toasts, as a salad in varieties of satay, and as an accompaniment to curries for clearing the palate after the rich, creamy curried coconut. It is easy and quick to prepare and its dressing can be kept refrigerated for a few weeks.

1/2 cup granulated sugar
1/2 cup rice vinegar or distilled vinegar
1 teaspoon salt
2 cups thinly sliced English cucumber
1/2 cup thinly sliced red onion or shallot, for garnish
2 sprigs chopped cilantro leaves for garnish
1 tablespoon shredded fresh red chilies,
    prik chee fa, or jalapeño (optional)

Preparation: In a small pot over medium heat, add the sugar, vinegar, and salt. Stir and cook until the mixture turns into a thin syrup, about 5 minutes. Let cool.

Stir in the sliced cucumber and onion. Transfer to a serving bowl and garnish with the cilantro and red chilies.

Eggplant Salad

This salad offers the unique flavor and texture of eggplant. Select an Asian green or purple long eggplant, as it has the right texture compared to a regular purple round eggplant, which has a less dense and mushy texture. The eggplant absorbs seasoning well and the tastes and flavors penetrate quickly throughout, as if it has been marinated for long time.

2 whole Thai long eggplants, *ma-kheua yao*,
  or Japanese eggplants
2 whole large red or yellow chilies,
  prik chee fa, serrano, or jalapeño
3 tablespoons vegetable oil
3 tablespoons thinly sliced shallot
1/2 cup ground lean pork
1/2 cup cleaned and deveined chopped shrimp
3 tablespoons fish sauce, more to taste
1 tablespoon palm sugar, more to taste
1/4 cup thinly sliced red onion
1 tablespoon finely chopped bird's-eye chilies
3 tablespoons lime juice, more to taste
2 tablespoons chopped green onion for garnish
2 tablespoons chopped cilantro leaves for garnish

Preparation: Grill the eggplants and chilies on open flame or roast in a 375°F oven, until done, about 7 to 10 minutes. Soak the grilled eggplant in cold water and peel off skins. Chop the eggplants and chilies into small pieces and set aside.

In a pan over medium heat, add the oil and cook the sliced shallot until light brown and crispy. Remove from the oil and set aside for garnish.

In the same pan, add the pork and break it down into smallest chunks. Stir in the shrimp and cook until done. Stir in the fish sauce and palm sugar; remove from the heat.

In a bowl, combine the eggplant, chilies, pork and shrimp mixture, red onion, bird's-eye chilies, and lime juice.

Transfer to a serving platter and sprinkle with the chopped green onion, cilantro, and fried shallot before serving.

Fish Cakes

The Central region has networks of natural and manmade rivers and canals, where freshwater fish grow plentifully. For cooking purposes, Thais categorize fish according to their flavors and textures. The best fish for this dish is *pla krai*, knife fish, whose meat has a certain degree of elasticity, and whose taste is most suitable for fish cakes. This recipe has been modified for use with any type of fresh white fish to yield a close resemblance to the hard-to-find *pla krai*. Conveniently, most Asian fish stores offer fishcake mix—a prepared blend of various fish, which is excellent for fish cakes and fish balls.

> 2 pounds fish fillets or fishcake mix
> 2 to 3 tablespoons Red Curry Paste (page 38)
> 2 tablespoons cornstarch
> 1 whole egg
> 4 very thinly shredded kaffir lime leaves
> 2 tablespoons fish sauce
> 1 tablespoon granulated sugar
> 1 cup thinly sliced long beans
> 3 cups vegetable oil for deep-frying

Preparation: In a food processor, combine all ingredients *except* the long beans and oil. Process until the mixture turns into a thick paste. Transfer to a bowl and fold in the long beans. Cover and refrigerate for at least 30 minutes.

In a deep pan, heat the oil to 350° to 375°F. With wet hands, form the fish paste into patties about 1 inch in diameter and 1/4 inch thick. Deep-fry the patties until golden brown on all sides, 4 to 6 minutes. Remove and drain over absorbent papers. Serve with the Dipping Sauce.

Dipping Sauce
2 tablespoons fish sauce
1/2 cup granulated sugar
1 cup sliced cucumber, peeled, seeded,
    and cut into crescents
1 cup thinly sliced red bell pepper
2 teaspoons finely minced garlic
1 teaspoon finely minced bird's-eye chilies (optional)
1/4 cup rice vinegar or lime juice
1/4 cup chopped roasted peanuts
1/4 teaspoon salt
5 sprigs cilantro leaves for garnish

Preparation: In a small pot over medium heat, combine 2 tablespoons water, the fish sauce, and sugar. Cook and stir until the sugar is dissolved and the mixture reduced into thin syrup. Remove from the heat and let cool.

Add the rest of the ingredients to the syrup and combine well. Serve as a sauce to the fish cakes.

This is a simple, quick recipe for cooking curry. The name *Chuchi*, I suspec
mimics a sizzling sound of "shoo" and "shee" as liquid hits a hot pan. Other
kinds of meat can be substituted for fish, and named accordingly, such as
Chuchi Neua for beef, *Chuchi Moo* for pork, etc. The same ingredients and
cooking methods may be used for all the meats.

> 2 cups coconut milk
> 3 tablespoons Gaeng Koa Curry Paste (page 32)
> 1/4 cup fish sauce
> 2 tablespoons palm sugar
> 1 pound fish fillet, sliced into bite-size pieces
> 1/8 cup green peppercorns, fresh or brined (optional)
> 1 cup shredded bamboo shoot (optional)
> 3 pieces kaffir lime leaves for garnish
> 1/8 cup shredded red chili or bell pepper for garnish
> 1/2 cup sweet basil leaf, *bai horapha* for garnish

Preparation: In a pan over medium heat, add 1/2 cup of the coconut milk.
Stir in the curry paste and cook until fragrant.

Add the remaining 1 1/2 cups coconut milk, fish sauce, and palm sugar; bring
the mixture to a boil. Add the fish, green peppercorns, and bamboo shoot if
using, to the pan and simmer until the fish is done, 7 to 10 minutes. The liquid should be somewhat evaporated and the sauce thickened.

Stack and roll the kaffir lime leaves tightly into a cigarette-like roll. Slice the
roll thinly and unravel into fine, long strips.

Arrange the fish on a serving platter and top with the sauce. Garnish with the
shredded kaffir lime leaves, red chili, and basil leaf before serving with
steamed rice.

Fried Eggs with Tamarind Sauce

Kai Look-Kuey

Serves 4

There is an intriguing story that goes along with this simple and minimalist dish. The name *"Kai Look-Kuey"* means son-in-law's eggs. During hard times, a man was expecting a visit from his in-laws. Having only short notice, he devised an elaborate dinner to impress them and show that he could take good care of their daughter. However, he had no provision other than eggs in his chicken coop and basic seasonings. With these limited ingredients, he came up with a wonderful and creative egg dish. The story ended well and the dish was delicious, served with steamed rice.

> 6 whole eggs
> 2 cups vegetable oil for deep-frying
> 1/2 cup very thinly sliced shallot for garnish

Preparation: Boil the eggs for 10 minutes until hard-boiled. Remove from the heat and let cool. Peel the eggs and set aside to dry.

In a saucepan, heat the oil to 350° to 375°F and fry the sliced shallot for 3 to 5 minutes until light brown and crispy. Set aside. With the same oil, fry the whole eggs until golden brown on all sides. Remove and drain over absorbent papers.

> **Tamarind Sauce**
> 1/2 cup tamarind liquid
> 1/2 cup fish sauce
> 1/4 cup palm sugar, more to taste

Preparation: Combine all ingredients in a saucepan, heat to a boil, and simmer for 5 to 10 minutes until the sauce turns syrupy.

To serve, cut the eggs in half lengthwise. Arrange the eggs on a serving platter, sprinkle with sauce and top with the deep-fried shallot. Serve the eggs with the remaining sauce on the side.

Fried Fish with Garlic and Pepper

If you love garlic, this dish is your ambrosia. A whole cooked fish is an impressive sight and will command respect from your guests, and its seductive taste will win them over. The fish is marinated and fried until golden brown, and toped with seasoned crispy garlic. Pork and beef can be prepared the same way, and fish sauce can be used instead of soy sauce as a flavor enhancer.

Marinade
1 whole fish, 2 to 2 1/2 pounds, scaled and cleaned
1 tablespoon finely minced garlic
5 whole finely minced fresh or
   dried bird's-eye chilies (optional)
1/2 tablespoon salt
1 tablespoon brandy or whisky
2 tablespoons plus 3 cups vegetable oil
3 tablespoons flour or tempura batter mix

Preparation: Cut 5 slashes on both sides of the fish almost to the bone.

Combine the garlic, chilies, salt, brandy, and 2 tablespoons oil; rub the mixture all over the fish. Marinate the fish for at least 1 hour. The marinade ingredients can also be combined roughly in a food processor. Do not process into a paste, it will burn when frying the fish.

Sprinkle the flour all over the fish. Heat 3 cups oil in a wok or large skillet, 350° to 375°F, and fry the fish until golden brown on both sides. Fry the fish longer if you prefer it crispy. Remove from the oil and drain. Set aside on a serving platter.

Sauce
2 tablespoons finely minced cilantro root or stem
1/4 cup very thinly sliced garlic
1 tablespoon coarsely ground black pepper
1/4 teaspoon salt
1/2 cup fish or chicken stock
2 tablespoons light soy sauce
1 tablespoon granulated sugar
1/4 cup chopped cilantro leaves for garnish
2 tablespoons shredded red chilies for garnish

Preparation: In a saucepan over medium heat, add 1/2 cup of the oil from frying fish and cook the cilantro root, garlic, black pepper, and salt until the garlic is light brown and crispy. Scoop and strain the garlic mixture out of the pan and set aside. Discard the oil.

Add the fish stock to the saucepan, cook until boiling then stir in the soy sauce and sugar. Pour the sauce over the fish and sprinkle with the fried garlic mixture. Garnish with fresh cilantro and red chilies before serving.

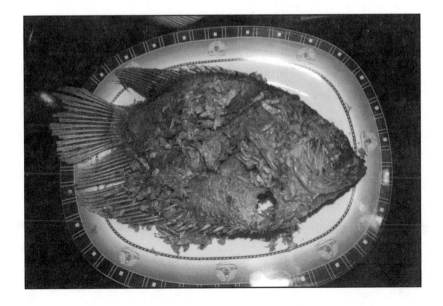

Fried Rice with Crab

This is my favorite fried rice of all time. Leftover rice is the most suitable starch for this dish for its semidried texture, which won't become mushy when fried. If using fresh steamed rice, spread the rice on a tray and refrigerate for 30 minutes to dry. It is a stir-fry dish, which takes few minutes to cook so all ingredients should be completely prepared in advance. Some recipes call for chopped fresh pineapple for a refreshing flavor.

3 tablespoons vegetable oil
2 tablespoons finely minced garlic
2 tablespoons chopped shallot
1 tablespoon finely minced cilantro root or stem
1 cup crabmeat
3 cups steamed rice
2 tablespoons fish sauce
2 tablespoons Maggi seasoning or light soy sauce
2 tablespoons granulated sugar
2 whole eggs, beaten
2 tablespoons chopped green onion
1 cup chopped fresh pineapple (optional)
1/2 teaspoon ground black pepper
2 tablespoons chopped cilantro leaves for garnish
1 whole lime, wedged, for accompaniment
1/2 cup sliced cucumber for accompaniment
1/2 cup sliced tomato for accompaniment

Preparation: In a wok or skillet over high heat, add the oil and cook the garlic, shallot, and cilantro root until fragrant. Add the crabmeat and stir to mix well.

Fluff the rice to fully separate and add to the wok. Stir in the fish sauce, Maggi seasoning, and sugar; stir-fry until well combined.

Create a well in the center of the wok, add some oil if it is too dry. Add the beaten eggs and scramble until firm. Sprinkle with the green onion, pineapple (if using), and ground pepper. Stir until all ingredients are well combined and heated through.

Transfer to serving plates and top with cilantro. Serve the fried rice with the accompaniments and Fish Sauce and Chili, *Nam Pla Prik* (page 31).

Fried Spring Rolls

The Chinese influence over Southeast Asia is so great that each country has eveloped its own kind of spring roll, created its own name for it, and embelshed it with its own local flavors. The Thai version is served with a spicy diping sauce or any ready-made condiment to spice it up.

1 cup dried vermicelli or glass noodles,
    soaked in warm water
1 cup ground lean pork
1 cup peeled and deveined chopped shrimp
1 cup shredded mushroom (your choice)
2 tablespoons very finely minced cilantro roots or stems
2 tablespoons very finely minced garlic
1 teaspoon ground pepper
2 tablespoons fish sauce
1 tablespoon Maggi seasoning
1 tablespoon granulated sugar
1/2 teaspoon salt
1 cup bean sprouts (optional)
1 package spring rolls, lumpia, or rice sheet wrapper, 4-inch square
3 cups vegetable oil for deep-frying

Preparation: Soak the noodles in warm water until soft, about 30 minutes, using several changes of water if necessary. Drain and cut into short strips; set aside.

In a bowl, combine the pork, shrimp, mushroom, cilantro, garlic, ground pepper, fish sauce, Maggi seasoning, sugar, and salt; mix well to make a stuffing.

Spread the wrappers and fill about 2 tablespoons of the stuffing at one end. Top with the noodles and bean sprouts, if using. Roll up, tuck both ends, and seal completely.

Heat the oil in a pan to 350°F to 375°F and fry the spring rolls until golden brown and crispy on all sides. Remove and drain on absorbent papers. Serve the spring rolls with Dipping Sauce.

–continued–

Dipping Sauce
1/4 cup rice or distilled white vinegar
1/2 cup granulated sugar
1 teaspoon salt
2 tablespoons fish sauce
1 tablespoon finely minced garlic
1 tablespoon chopped mild red chilies, *prik chee fa*, serrano, or jalapeño
2 tablespoons chopped roasted peanuts

Preparation: Combine all ingredients and stir until the sugar is dissolved.

Galangal Chicken Soup

Tom Kha Gai

Galangal provides such a unique flavor that it cannot be substituted. It is widely available in fresh, dried, and frozen forms in Asian grocery stores. This recipe highlights the best and most popular use of the herb, paring it with coconut milk and chicken meat. The combined aromatic creamy soup with its refreshing sweet and sour taste makes the dish one of the top ten choices of both Thais and lovers of Thai food.

3 cups chicken stock
6 pieces fresh galangal,
   sliced 1/8 inch thick x 2 inches x 2 inches
2 stalks lemongrass, tender part,
   cut into 2-inch-long pieces and bruised
4 pieces kaffir lime leaves
2 tablespoons sliced shallot, 1/4-inch thick
2 cups diced chicken, 1/4-inch cubes
3 cups bite-size straw mushrooms (or other mushrooms)
2 cups coconut milk
1/4 cup fish sauce, more to taste
2 tablespoons granulated sugar
1 tablespoon chicken bouillon
1/4 cup lime juice, more to taste
1 teaspoon chopped bird's-eye chili, more or less to taste
2 tablespoons chopped cilantro leaf for garnish
2 tablespoons chopped green onion for garnish

Preparation: In a medium pot, bring the stock to a boil and then add the galangal, lemongrass, and kaffir leaves. Cook for 10 minutes until the broth is reduced to 1/2 to 1/4 the original volume. Discard the solids or leave them in for stronger flavor.

Add the shallot, chicken, and mushrooms; cook until the chicken is done. Add the coconut milk, fish sauce, sugar, and chicken bouillon. Bring the mixture to a boil one more time and remove from the heat.

Add the lime juice and bird's-eye chili. Adjust the taste by adding more fish sauce and lime juice. Garnish with the cilantro and green onion before serving.

Glass Noodle Salad

This is a noodle dish that has been transformed into a salad. Glass noodles are made from mung beans and when cooked, turn glassy clear. After being tossed with dressing, they maintain an elastic texture without disintegrating, as do other noodles. Like most Thai salads, the lime taste dominates this refreshing dish.

5 ounces dried cellophane or glass noodles, *woon sen*
1 cup dried mouse's-ear mushrooms
   (or 2 cups other fresh mushrooms)
3 tablespoons vegetable oil
2 tablespoons thinly sliced shallot for garnish
1/8 cup dried shrimp (optional)
2 tablespoons minced garlic
1 cup ground lean pork
1 cup peeled and deveined prawns
3/4 cup thinly sliced red onion
1 cup thinly sliced Chinese celery, stems and leaves
5 tablespoons lime juice, more to taste
1/4 cup fish sauce, more to taste
2 tablespoons granulated sugar, more to taste
1 tablespoon minced bird's-eye chilies,
   more or less to taste
1 cup julienne red bell pepper for garnish
1/4 cup chopped roasted peanuts for garnish
2 tablespoons chopped cilantro leaves for garnish
2 tablespoons chopped green onion for garnish

Preparation: In a pot, bring 4 cups water to a boil and add the noodles. Cook and stir to separate the noodles until tender for 5 minutes. Drain and rinse with cold water. Cut the noodles into 6-inch strains with shears or a knife; set aside.

Soak the mushrooms in warm water until fully expanded, about 15 minutes. Rinse and slice into thin strips; set aside.

a pan over medium heat, add the oil and fry the shallot until light brown
d crispy. Remove and drain over absorbent papers. With the same oil, fry the
ied shrimp until golden brown; remove and set aside.

the same pan, add the garlic and cook until fragrant. Stir in the pork,
awns, and mushrooms and cook until done; set aside. Alternatively, the pork,
awns, and mushrooms can be poached in boiling water with little salt.

a large bowl, combine all ingredients *except* the garnishes. Adjust the taste
ith more fish sauce, lime juice, and sugar.

ansfer to a serving platter and top with the garnishes. Serve with fresh veg-
ables such as cabbage and lettuce on the side.

This popular soup distinguishes itself with a pungent green curry and sweet coconut milk, as the name implies; *keow* is green and *wan* is sweet. The dish is usually served with jasmine rice but the Thais enjoy eating it equally with a rice noodle called *Kanom Jeen*. Beef can be substituted or even seafood such as firm fresh fish and shellfish. As most seafood cooks very fast, it should be added last, perhaps even a couple minutes before serving.

> 2 tablespoons vegetable oil
> 3 tablespoons Green Curry Paste (page 34)
> 2 cups diced chicken, 1/2-inch cubes
> 3 cups coconut milk
> 2 cups diced Thai or Japanese eggplants,
>   1/2-inch cubes
> 2 cups diced zucchini, 1/2-inch cubes
> 1 cup julienned red bell pepper
> 6 whole kaffir lime leaves
> 1/4 cup fish sauce, more to taste
> 3 tablespoons palm sugar, more to taste
> 1 tablespoon chicken bouillon
> 2 sprigs sweet basil leaves, *bai horapha* for garnish
> 1/4 cup julienned red jalapeño or
>   red bell pepper for garnish

Preparation: In a pot over medium heat, add the oil and cook the green curry paste until fragrant. Stir in the chicken and cook with the curry for 3 minutes. Add the coconut milk and bring the mixture to a boil. Do not let it boil over.

Add the vegetables, kaffir lime leaves, fish sauce, sugar, and chicken bouillon. Continue simmering for 7 to 10 minutes until the chicken and vegetables are done.

Adjust the taste by adding more fish sauce and sugar. Sprinkle with the basil and jalapeño for garnish before serving.

This fresh salad is an accumulation of many cuisines: Chinese, Indian, Indonesian, and now American. Many types of fresh and cooked vegetable provide a variety of flavors and textures. Sweet and sour are dominant tastes for its creamy and nutty curry dressing.

> 1/2 pound chicken breast
> 2 cups bean sprouts
> 1 head lettuce, cut to bite-size pieces
> 1 cup thinly sliced English cucumber
> 1/2 cup thinly sliced red onion
> 1/2 cup seeded julienned tomato
> 1 cup thinly sliced fried tofu
> 3 eggs, hard-boiled and sliced
> 1 (6-ounce) bag unsalted potato chips

Preparation: In a pot, bring 2 cups water to a boil and poach the chicken until done, 5 to 7 minutes. Remove and shred into thin, long strips. Divide the chicken into 2 portions: 3/4 and 1/4 of the amount, set aside.

In the same pot, poach the bean sprouts until tender for 2 minutes. Remove and set aside to drain.

Arrange the prepared vegetables on a serving tray. Top with the sliced tofu, eggs, 3/4-portion of the shredded chicken, and potato chips. Serve with the dressing on the side.

Peanut Dressing
6 whole dried large red chilies, *prik chee fa*,
   serrano, jalapeño, or California chili
1/4 cup chopped shallot
1 tablespoon chopped garlic
2 teaspoons ground coriander
2 teaspoons ground cumin

–continued–

1 cup coconut milk
1/4 cup palm sugar
1/4 cup fish sauce
1/4 cup tamarind liquid
1/2 cup chunky peanut butter
1 cup coconut cream

Preparation: Seed and soak the dried chilies in warm water until soft. Drain and squeeze dry. In a mortar with pestle or food processor, process the chilies, shallot, garlic, coriander, cumin, and the remaining 1/4-portion shredded chicken until they form a smooth paste.

In a pot over medium heat, add 1/2 cup of coconut milk. Stir in the paste and cook until fragrant.

Add the remaining 1/2 cup coconut milk, palm sugar, fish sauce, tamarind liquid, and peanut butter. Stir constantly until the mixture is well mixed and bring it to a boil. Add the coconut cream and remove from the heat.

To serve, portion the salad onto serving plates and sprinkle with the dressing.

The Best of Regional Thai Cuisine

Hot & Sour Prawn Soup

Tom Yum Goong

Serves 6

Tom Yum is the most common dish cooked in Thai households, where most fresh herbs and spices can be gathered from the backyard garden. It is quick and easy to prepare, and any seasoning can be added at any time, according to taste. If all else fails and you are in a time crunch, *Tom Yum* can save your day. Besides prawns, beef, pork, and fish are all suitable for this dish.

1 pound prawns, shelled and deveined, reserve the shells
1 tablespoon shrimp bouillon
   (plus 2 tablespoons, optional)
2 stalks lemongrass, tender part,
   cut into 2-inch-long pieces and bruised
3 pieces thinly sliced galangal
5 pieces kaffir lime leaves
1 tablespoon chopped garlic or pickled garlic
2 tablespoons sliced shallot
3 cups straw mushrooms (or other mushrooms)
1/4 cup fish sauce, more to taste
1 tablespoon chili paste with soybean oil,
   namprik pow (see glossary)
5 whole bird's-eye chilies, bruised, more or less to taste
1/4 cup lime juice, more to taste
2 tablespoons chopped cilantro for garnish
2 tablespoons chopped green onion for garnish

Preparation: To make 4 cups of shellfish stock, boil the prawn shells in a pot with 5 cups of water for 10 minutes. Strain the broth and discard the shells. Or dilute 2 tablespoons of shrimp bouillon with 4 cups of water to make the stock.

In a pot, bring the stock to a boil and add the lemongrass, galangal, kaffir lime, garlic, and shallot. Cook for 5 minutes and then add the mushrooms, fish sauce, shrimp bouillon, and chili paste.

Bring the stock to a boil again and add the prawns, cook until done for 2 minutes. Do not overcook the prawns.

Remove from the heat and then add the bird's-eye chilies and lime juice. Adjust the taste with more fish sauce, lime juice, and chili paste. Portion the soup into serving bowls and garnish with the cilantro and green onion before serving.

Hunter Soup with Shrimp
Gaeng Paa Goong Kup Het

Serves 4

Every cuisine seems to have its own so-called hunter dish, since the hunter also has to eat (some are even good cooks). This version is easy to prepare and delivers a surprising hearty soup full of aromatic flavors. The hunter usually prefers wild boar meat, but pork is a good substitute, with long beans as a complementary vegetable.

1 pound shrimp or prawns,
  peeled and deveined, shells reserved
1 tablespoon shrimp bouillon (optional)
2 tablespoons vegetable oil
3 tablespoons Hunter (Gaeng Paa) Curry Paste (page 35)
3 cups sliced straw mushrooms, bite-size
  (or other mushrooms)
2 tablespoons fish sauce, more to taste
4 whole kaffir limes
1/2 cup holy basil leaf, *bai krapow*
1/4 cup shredded red pepper for garnish

Preparation: Peel and clean the fresh shrimp or prawns and save the shells for stock. Boil the shells with 3 cups of water for 10 minutes and strain to get 2 cups stock. Or dilute the shrimp bouillon with 2 cups of water to make the stock.

In a pot over medium heat, add the oil and cook the curry paste until fragrant. Add the shrimp and cook until almost done for 2 minutes.

Add the stock to the pot and bring to a boil. Add the mushrooms, fish sauce, and kaffir limes. Bring to a boil one more time. Adjust the taste with more fish sauce.

Sprinkle with the basil leaf and shredded red pepper. Remove from the heat and serve with steamed rice.

Massamun Beef Curry

Dating back to the ancient kingdom of Ayudthaya, King Narai, who was fond of Indian food, imported a chef for his royal kitchen. From the royal court, the aromatic Massamun curry made it into the mainstream Thai diet, and its paste still contains an extraordinary variety of Indian herbs and spices. Meat must be slow cooked and tenderized to the point of melting in your mouth. Chicken drumsticks are also a popular meat choice.

4 cups coconut milk
1 pound top or bottom round steak,
   diced into 1/2-inch cubes
3 whole cardamom seeds
3 whole bay leaves
1 piece cinnamon stick
1/2 pound small new potatoes, peeled
1/2 pound pearl onions, peeled
1 cup coconut cream
1/4 cup Massamun Curry Paste (page 36)
1/2 cup roasted whole peanuts
1 1/2 cups diced pineapple, 1/2-inch cubes (optional)
1/2 cup tamarind liquid
1/4 cup fish sauce, more to taste
3 tablespoons palm sugar, more to taste

Preparation: In a pot over medium heat, combine 2 cups of the coconut milk, diced beef, cardamom, bay leaves, and cinnamon; bring the mixture to a boil and reduce the heat to simmer. Continue cooking for 20 to 30 minutes until the beef is tender.

Cook the potatoes and onions in boiling water for 5 minutes until almost done. Drain and set aside. Do not overcook or they will fall apart.

In a pot over medium heat, add 1/2 cup of coconut cream. Stir in the curry paste and cook until fragrant. Add the remaining 2 cups coconut milk, and the tenderized beef and its liquid.

Bring the mixture to a boil and then add the rest of the ingredients. Continue cooking until the potatoes and onions are completely done for 5 minutes. Adjust the taste with more fish sauce and sugar before serving.

Mini Purses

This dish is a true appetizer, whereas most Thai appetizers can be eaten as a meal with rice. To achieve the appealing presentation of little purses with tie strings is a time-consuming, delicate process. But the end product, both in appearance and taste, will impress anyone, including you.

Stuffing
1 cup ground pork
1 cup shrimp, cleaned and deveined
1 tablespoon minced garlic
1 tablespoon minced cilantro root or stem
1 tablespoon minced shallot
1 whole egg
1 tablespoon soy sauce
1 tablespoon fish sauce
1 tablespoon granulated sugar
1/4 teaspoon ground pepper
1 tablespoon shrimp or chicken bouillon
1/2 cup chopped water chestnut
1/4 cup chopped cilantro leaves
2 tablespoons cornstarch

Preparation: In a blender or food processor, process all ingredients with several pauses until well mixed but *not* in a smooth paste.

Wrapper and Tie
1 bunch garlic chives or leek for string ties
1 package thin wonton wrappers
4 cups vegetable oil for deep-frying

Preparation: Trim the chives or leek, using the leafy, green portion only. For the leek, slice into thin, long strips. Poach the chives or leek strips in boiling water momentarily to soften up and rinse with cold water.

Fill a wonton wrapper with 3/4 teaspoon of stuffing and pull all corners up to form a little purse. Tie and secure the purse with a chive or leek string. Continue the process until the stuffing has been used up.

Heat the oil in a deep pan to 375°F and deep-fry the purses until golden brown. Serve with the Thai Sweet Chili Sauce or Chinese White Plum Sauce (see glossary).

Morning Glory with Peanut Curry

This elaborate dish carries the name of a leading male character, Pra Ram in a classical Thai myth. He has an emerald green complexion and is represented by morning glory, a green vegetable in this dish. Pra Ram performs an ablution, *Loung Soung*, and emerges fresh and clean with anointment as the morning glory is poached and topped with a golden curry sauce.

Chili Paste
4 whole dried large red chilies, *prik chee fa*, serrano, jalapeño, or California chili
1 tablespoon chopped garlic
2 tablespoons chopped shallot
2 teaspoons chopped cilantro root or stem
1 tablespoon chopped lemongrass, tender part
1 teaspoon chopped galangal
1 teaspoon chopped kaffir lime rind or leaf
1 teaspoon salt

Preparation: Seed and soak the dried chili in water until soft. Drain and squeeze dry. In a mortar with pestle or food processor, process all ingredients until they form a smooth paste; set aside.

2 pounds morning glory or spinach
1 pound beef tenderloin
2 1/2 cups coconut milk
3 tablespoons tamarind liquid
2 tablespoons palm sugar, more to taste
2 tablespoons fish sauce, more to taste
1/2 cup chunky peanut butter
3 tablespoons chopped roasted peanuts for garnish

Preparation: Wash the morning glory and trim off the root. Cut into 2-inch-long pieces and poach in boiling water for 2 minutes. Remove and plunge into cold water immediately. Drain to dry and arrange on a serving platter.

Slice the beef across the grain into thin, 2-inch-long pieces. Poach in boiling water until almost done for 3 minutes. Remove and arrange on top of the morning glory.

In a pot over medium heat, add 1/2 cup of coconut milk and stir in the chili paste; cook until fragrant. Add the remaining 2 cups coconut milk, tamarind liquid, sugar, and fish sauce.

Bring the mixture to a boil and stir in the peanut butter. Cook and stir constantly until the peanut butter is dissolved and mixed well. Remove from the heat.

To serve, heat the morning glory and beef in a microwave and pour the peanut sauce over the beef. Sprinkle with the chopped peanuts before serving.

Pandan Leaf Wrapped Chicken

Pandan is a tropical bush with long, thin blade-like leaves that have a strong sweet fragrance. Its whole leaves are used for flower arrangements, fragrant food wrappers, and hanging air fresheners. Its extract adds a sweet fragrance to many Thai desserts, much like vanilla does.

2 pounds boneless, skinless chicken breast
2 teaspoons chopped cilantro root or stem
1 teaspoon ground pepper
2 tablespoons chopped garlic
2 tablespoons light soy sauce
2 tablespoons Maggi seasoning
1 tablespoon chicken bouillon
2 tablespoons granulated sugar
1 teaspoon salt
3/4 cup coconut milk or milk
2 tablespoons brandy
1 tablespoon sesame oil
1 bunch pandan leaves, about 30 leaves
4 cups vegetable oil for frying
1 bottle *Sriracha* sauce for accompaniment

Preparation: Dice the chicken into 1-inch cubes; set aside.

In a mortar with pestle or a food processor, process the cilantro root, ground pepper, and garlic until they form a smooth paste. Transfer the mixture into a bowl and mix in the soy sauce, Maggi seasoning, chicken bouillon, sugar, salt, coconut milk, brandy, and sesame oil. Stir in the diced chicken and marinate for at least 30 minutes.

Clean and separate the pandan leaves into individual long pieces. Wrap each diced chicken with a leaf and loop both ends into a knot to secure. Continue the process until all chicken has been wrapped up.

Heat the oil in a deep skillet and fry the wrapped chicken until golden brown, about 5 to 10 minutes. Or preheat an oven to 375°F and bake the wrapped chicken until golden brown, about 15 minutes. Serve the chicken with the *Sriracha* sauce (see glossary) on the side.

This is another salad that satisfies the refined tastes of the people in the central region. This version uses sour and sweet as the principal flavors; fresh poached seafood such as prawns can top the dish to heighten its status. Roasted peanuts provide extra texture and crunchiness as a perfect addition to this popular dish.

> 1 green papaya (about 2 pounds)
> 1 whole carrot
> 1 tablespoon chopped garlic
> 1 tablespoon minced bird's-eye chilies,
>   more or less to taste
> 2 tablespoons dried shrimp
> 1/4 cup sliced long beans, 2-inch long
> 1/2 cup seeded, sliced tomato
> 3 tablespoons chopped roasted peanuts
> 1/4 cup lime juice, more to taste
> 1/4 cup fish sauce, more to taste
> 2 tablespoons palm sugar, more to taste
> 1 head cabbage or lettuce for accompaniment

Preparation: Peel and seed the papaya. Rinse with water and shred into fine strains with a shredder or knife, to make 2 cups. Peel and shred the carrot to make 1 cup.

In a clay mortar with pestle, crush the garlic first then crush the chilies, then shrimp, and long beans until well mixed.

Add the papaya, carrot, and tomato and work the pestle until the mixture is well combined. Add the peanuts, lime juice, fish sauce, and sugar; continue crushing to mix well so the mixture absorbs all flavors.

Taste the salad and adjust the taste with more fish sauce, lime juice, and sugar. Serve with fresh vegetables such as cabbage and lettuce.

Satay is not complete without peanut sauce. This sweet, creamy curry sauce adds complexity to the simple skewered barbecued meat. You can control the amount of heat by slowly adding the chili and testing it along the way. Using ground peanuts or peanut butter yields almost identical results.

6 whole dried large red chilies, *prik chee fa*,
   serrano, jalapeño, or California chili
1 teaspoon whole cumin seeds
2 teaspoons whole coriander seeds
2 teaspoons chopped shallot
1 tablespoon chopped garlic
1 tablespoon chopped lemongrass, tender part
2 teaspoons chopped galangal
1 teaspoon chopped kaffir lime skin or leaves
1 teaspoon shrimp paste
2 teaspoons salt
2 1/2 cups coconut milk
3/4 cup coarsely ground peanuts or
   chunky peanut butter
1/2 cup palm sugar

Preparation: Seed the dried chilies and soak in warm water until soft. Drain and squeeze dry. Dry roast the cumin and coriander seeds in a pan over a stove until fragrant, about 5 to 7 minutes.

In a mortar with pestle or food processor, process the chilies, cumin, coriander, shallot, garlic, lemongrass, galangal, kaffir lime, shrimp paste, and salt until they form a smooth paste.

In a pot over medium heat, add 1/2 cup of coconut milk and cook the paste until fragrant. Add the remaining 2 cups coconut milk, peanuts, and sugar; cook for 3 minutes, stirring constantly.

Remove from the heat and serve the sauce on the side with the satay and accompany with Cucumber Salad, *Ajad* (page 98).

Pineapple Coconut Noodles

My favorite childhood dish was an offering off the shoulder of a wandering merchant. Its taste of sweet, creamy coconut and refreshing pineapple explodes in your mouth. On a hot day or on any day, this fresh dish with mint leaves will calm you down.

Coconut Sauce
1 pound chopped white fish fillet
1/2 teaspoon salt
3 cups coconut milk
3 cups coconut cream

Preparation: Poach the fish in 4 cups boiling water until done, about 5 minutes. Drain and break the fish into small chunks.

Bring the coconut milk to a boil, add the fish and salt; stir to mix well. Bring the mixture to a boil and add the coconut cream. Cook to almost boiling; remove from the heat, and let cool.

14 ounces rice noodles, *kanom jeen*,
  or Japanese somen
2 cups diced fresh pineapple, 1/4-inch cubes
1/4 cup finely shredded fresh ginger
1/8 cup thinly sliced garlic
1 cup shredded or pounded dried shrimp
3 hard-boiled eggs, thinly sliced
2 tablespoons chopped bird's-eye chilies,
  more or less to taste
1/4 cup chopped fresh mint leaves
1/2 cup fish sauce
1/2 cup lime juice
1/2 cup granulated sugar

Preparation: Cook the noodles in 6 cups boiling water until tender. Drain and rinse with cold water. Portion the noodles into small wads, each about the size of a small bird's nest, and set aside. You should have about 12 to 18 wads.

–continued–

To serve, place 2 to 3 wads of noodles in a serving plate, pour 3/4 cup of the coconut sauce over the noodles and top with 1/3 cup pineapple. Sprinkle with the ginger, garlic, dried shrimp, sliced eggs, chopped chilies, and mint leaves.

Sprinkle on the sugar, lime juice, and fish sauce before serving.

Pineapple Coconut Curry

Gaeng Koa Supparod

Pineapple, coconut, and curry are a perfect combination that will awaken your taste buds. Sweet, sour, creamy, and spicy are balanced in this refreshing yet hearty dish. Instead of beef, chicken, pork, prawn, or any combination are delightful substitutes.

2 tablespoons vegetable oil
3 tablespoons Gaeng Kua Curry Paste (page 32)
2 cups diced beef tenderloin, cut into 1/2-inch cubes
3 cups coconut milk
3 cups diced pineapple, cut into 1/2-inch cubes
1/4 cup julienned red bell pepper
3 tablespoons fish sauce
2 tablespoons palm sugar
1 tablespoons beef bouillon
Salt to taste
2 sprigs sweet basil leaves, *bai horapha*, for garnish

Preparation: In a pot over medium heat, add the oil and cook the curry paste until fragrant. Add the beef and stir until well coated. Add the coconut milk and cook for 7 to 10 minutes until the beef is tender.

Add the pineapple, bell pepper, fish sauce, sugar, and beef bouillon. Increase the heat and cook for 5 minutes more. Season with salt to taste.

Sprinkle with the basil leaves for garnish before serving.

Pomelo Salad with Beef

Pomelo is a giant grapefruit that comes in U.S. markets in late winter, but in Thailand, *som oo* is available year-round. There are two varieties of pomelo: white meat and pink meat. Both varieties are truly sweet but one has a hint of sour. The pink pomelo is suitable for the salad because the sweet and sour intensifies the flavor. Prawns can be used instead of the beef.

3 tablespoons vegetable oil
3 tablespoons very thinly sliced shallot
    for garnish
3 tablespoons dried shrimp
    for garnish (optional)
1/2 pound beef tenderloin,
    sliced thin into bite-size pieces
1/4 cup grated coconut or
    coconut flakes for garnish
2 cups pomelo, peeled, seeded,
    and broken into small pieces
1/2 cup thinly sliced red onion
1 cup julienned colored bell pepper
1 head lettuce
2 tablespoons chopped cilantro leaves for garnish
2 tablespoons chopped green onion for garnish

Preparation: In a pan over medium heat, add the oil and fry the sliced shallot and dried shrimp, one at a time, until light brown and crispy. Remove from the oil and set aside for garnish.

In the same pan, cook the sliced beef to your desired doneness and set aside. Or poach the beef in boiling water.

Roast the grated coconut in a dry pan over a stove or in an oven until light brown and fragrant, about 5 to 7 minutes. Set aside.

Dressing
1/8 cup fish sauce
1/8 cup lime juice
1/8 cup orange or citrus juice
1 teaspoon very finely minced garlic
1 tablespoon chili paste with
   soybean oil, *namprik pow* (see glossary)
1 tablespoon granulated sugar
1 teaspoon chopped bird's-eye chili,
   more or less to taste

Preparation: Combine all ingredients and stir to mix well.

To serve, combine the beef, pomelo, red onion, and bell pepper; gently toss, adding a little dressing at a time and taste. Adjust the taste by adding more dressing.

Transfer onto a serving platter on a bed of lettuce and sprinkle with the chopped cilantro, green onion, fried shallot, fried shrimp, and roasted coconut.

Pork is the most popular meat in Thai satay. Two out of three restaurants serve only pork satay because the meat is tender, easy to handle, inexpensive, and quick to absorb a marinade. In the old days, customers would sit in front of a charcoal grill with a bowl of peanut sauce and cucumber salad. Merchants would serve them as many fresh grilled skewered satays as they wanted or could eat. The number of wooden skewers from each person would be counted to settle the bills. Eating in a proper increment (20, 30, 40) showed courtesy and made for easy calculation.

Marinade
2 teaspoons ground coriander
1 teaspoon ground cumin
1 teaspoon very finely minced galangal
2 tablespoons very finely minced lemongrass, tender part
1 tablespoon ground turmeric
1 teaspoon salt
1 teaspoon ground pepper
1 tablespoon fish sauce
1 tablespoon granulated sugar
3/4 cup coconut cream
1 pound lean pork
50 bamboo skewers

Preparation: Process the coriander, cumin, galangal, lemongrass, turmeric, salt, and pepper in a mortar with pestle or in a food processor until they form a smooth paste. Add the fish sauce, sugar, and coconut cream; process until well mixed.

Cut the pork into thin slices about 1 inch wide and 6 inches long. Combine the meat with marinade thoroughly and refrigerate for at least 2 hours.

Soak the bamboo skewers in water to prevent them from burning and skewer the pork strips lengthwise.

Start a firewood or charcoal grill ahead of time to get medium heat. Grill the pork about 3 minutes on each side until done. Brush the meat occasionally with the remaining marinade. Serve the satay with Peanut Sauce (page 124) and Cucumber Salad, *Ajad* (page 98).

Try this dish as something different for breakfast, as Thai people do for special occasions. It also makes a delicious French-influenced appetizer. See Shrimp Toasts (page 137) for an alternative.

> 10 slices bread
> 1 1/2 cups ground lean pork (1 pound)
> 1 whole egg, beaten
> 3 tablespoons light soy sauce
> 1 tablespoon granulated sugar
> 1 teaspoon finely chopped cilantro root or stem
> 1/2 teaspoon ground pepper
> 2 tablespoons finely chopped garlic
> 6 sprigs cilantro leaves for garnish
> 1/2 cup finely sliced red bell pepper, for garnish
> 4 cups vegetable oil for frying

Preparation: Use dried old bread or toast or roast new bread lightly in an oven. The dried bread fries well and absorbs less oil.

In a food processor, combine the pork, half of the egg, soy sauce, sugar, 2 tablespoons water, cilantro root, ground pepper, and garlic. Process the mixture with several pauses until well mixed but *not* in a fine paste.

Cut the bread into quarters and spread about 1 tablespoon of the pork mixture over each quarter. Brush the remaining egg over the pork mixture and decorate with the cilantro leaves and shredded red bell pepper.

In a deep pan, heat the oil to 350° to 375°F and fry the bread with the spread side downward until golden brown. Remove from the oil and drain on absorbent papers. Serve the pork toast with Cucumber Salad, *Ajad* (page 98).

Red Curry Chicken

Red curry is the most versatile paste in Thai cooking. Many dishes, soups, stir-fries, and sauces are derived from red curry paste combined with any meat and vegetable. On holy days, monks in Buddhist monasteries often find the meal offerings comprised of three or four kinds of red curry dishes.

> 3 cups coconut milk
> 2 to 3 tablespoons Red Curry Paste (page 38)
> 1 1/2 cups diced chicken meat, 1/2-inch cubes
> 3 tablespoons fish sauce, more to taste
> 2 tablespoons palm sugar, more to taste
> 3 whole kaffir lime leaves
> 2 cups diced Thai eggplant or
>   Chinese eggplant, 1/2-inch cubes
>   (or shredded bamboo shoots or
>   green peas or combination)
> 2 red jalapeños, shredded, for garnish
> 1/2 cup sweet basil leaves, *bai horapha*, for garnish

Preparation: In a pot over medium heat, combine 1/2 cup of the coconut milk with the curry paste and cook until fragrant. Stir in the chicken and cook until done.

Add the remaining 2 1/2 cups coconut milk and stir in the fish sauce, palm sugar, and kaffir lime leaves. Bring the mixture almost to a boil and then add the eggplant. Continue cooking until the eggplant is done, about 5 to 7 minutes.

Before serving, garnish with the red peppers and basil leaves.

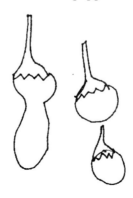

eafood Hot and Sour Soup

Pou is a stationary trap that dots the shallow part of the sea in the Gulf of Thailand. Fish can get in but cannot get out. Likewise, *Pou Tak*, broken trap, athers all the escaped fish into this soup. You can select your favorite seafood or the dish and adjust the seasonings to suit your palate.

6 cups shellfish stock
3 stalks lemongrass, tender part,
    cut into 2-inch-long pieces and bruised
3 pieces galangal, sliced 1/8-inch thick
4 whole kaffir lime leaves
1 tablespoon shrimp bouillon
3 tablespoons fish sauce, more to taste
1 tablespoon granulated sugar
1/2 cup prawns, peeled and deveined
1/2 cup mussels, cleaned
1/2 cup diced firm flesh fish, 1/2-inch cubes
1/2 cup cleaned diced squid, 1/2-inch cubes
2 cups sliced mushrooms, 1/4-inch thick
1/4 cup fresh lime juice, more to taste
1 tablespoon minced bird's-eye chilies,
    more or less to taste
2 tablespoons chopped green onion for garnish
2 tablespoons chopped cilantro for garnish

Preparation: In a pot, bring the stock to a boil and add the lemongrass, galangal, and kaffir leaves. Simmer for at least 10 minutes. Add the shrimp bouillon, fish sauce, and sugar; stir to mix well.

ust couple minutes before serving, bring the mixture to a boil and add the eafood and mushrooms. Cook for 3 to 5 minutes until the seafood and mushrooms are done. Remove from the heat and add the lime juice and chilies.

Adjust the taste with more fish sauce and lime juice. Sprinkle with the green onion and cilantro before serving.

People in the Central region have taken the simple *Tod Mun*, fried meat patty, and made many hybrids of it. Different kinds of meat in *Tod Mun* yield different tastes and textures to serve diverse palates. This shrimp cake recipe i very mild compared to the next, spicy recipe.

> 1 pound cleaned, deveined, and chopped shrimp
> 1/3 pound ground pork (optional)
> 1/2 teaspoon salt
> 1 tablespoon fish sauce
> 1 tablespoon Maggi seasoning
> 1 tablespoon granulated sugar
> 1/4 teaspoon ground white pepper
> 1 cup bread crumbs
> 3 cups vegetable oil for deep-frying
> 2 cups sliced fresh pineapple (optional)

Preparation: Combine the shrimp, pork, salt, fish sauce, Maggi seasoning, sugar, and pepper; knead until thickened and well mixed.

Wet your hands and roll about 1 tablespoon of the shrimp mixture into a round ball. Press the ball into a 1/4-inch-thick round cake and bread with the bread crumbs. Repeat the process and use up all the mixture.

Heat the oil in a deep pan to 350° to 375°F and fry the shrimp cakes until golden brown on both sides about 6 minutes. Remove from the pan and drair over absorbent papers.

Serve the shrimp cakes over the thinly sliced pineapple with Chinese White Plum Sauce, *Nam Jim Giem Boi* (see glossary), on the side.

Shrimp Cakes II (Spicy)

Spicy shrimp cakes are an alternative to the previous recipe, yielding an even more complex shrimp flavor. Compare the two and enjoy these simple, delicious appetizers.

2 pounds shrimp, peeled and deveined
2 to 3 tablespoons Red Curry Paste (page 38)
2 tablespoons cornstarch
1 whole egg
5 very thinly shredded kaffir lime leaves
2 tablespoons fish sauce
1 tablespoon granulated sugar
1 cup thinly sliced long beans
3 cups vegetable oil for deep-frying

Preparation: In a food processor, combine all ingredients *except* the long beans and oil. Process and pause repeatedly until well mixed but *not* into a fine paste. Transfer to a bowl and fold in the long beans. Refrigerate for at least 30 minutes.

In a deep pan, heat the oil to 350° to 375°F. With wet hands, form the paste into patties, each about 1 inch in diameter and 1/4 inch thick. Deep-fry the patties until golden brown on all sides, 4 to 6 minutes. Remove from the oil and drain over absorbent papers.

Dipping Sauce
2 tablespoons fish sauce
1/2 cup granulated sugar
1 cup peeled, seeded, and thinly sliced cucumber
1 cup thinly sliced red bell pepper
2 teaspoons finely minced garlic
1 teaspoon minced bird's-eye chilies, more or less to taste
1/4 cup rice vinegar or lime juice
1/4 cup chopped roasted peanuts
1/4 teaspoon salt
5 sprigs cilantro leaves for garnish

–continued–

Preparation: In a small pot over medium heat, combine 1/8 cup water, the fish sauce, and sugar. Cook and stir until the mixture is reduced to syrup, about 5 to 7 minutes. Remove from the heat and let cool. Before serving, add the rest of the ingredients to the syrup and combine well. Serve as the sauce to the shrimp cakes.

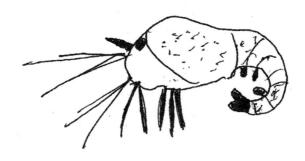

Shrimp Toasts

This appetizer has a French influence, but the added meat, herbs, and spices suit the Thai palate. It has a mild flavor and is often served for breakfast. See Pork Toasts (page 131) for an alternative.

    8 slices bread
    1/2 pound shrimp, peeled and deveined
    1 whole egg
    1 teaspoon chopped cilantro root or stem
    1 tablespoon chopped garlic
    1/4 teaspoon ground white pepper
    2 teaspoons light soy sauce
    1 tablespoon Maggi seasoning
    1 tablespoon granulated sugar
    2 tablespoons black and white sesame seeds
    3 cups vegetable oil for deep-frying

Preparation: Use dried old bread or toast or roast new bread lightly in an oven. The dried bread fries well and absorbs less oil.

In a food processor, combine the shrimp, egg, cilantro root, garlic, pepper, soy sauce, Maggi seasoning, and sugar. Process the mixture until well mixed but *not* into a fine paste.

Spread the mixture evenly over the pieces of bread and sprinkle with sesame seeds. Cut the bread into quarters.

Heat the oil in a deep pan to 350° to 375°F and fry the bread with the shrimp spread side downward until golden brown. Remove from the oil and drain over absorbent papers.

Serve the shrimp toast with Jam Sauce or Chinese White Plum Sauce (see glossary).

–continued–

Jam or Marmalade Sauce
1/4 cup fruit jam, marmalade, or preserves
1/4 cup rice vinegar
1/4 teaspoon salt

Preparation: In a small pot over medium heat, combine all ingredients and stir to mix well. Transfer to a bowl and serve with the shrimp toast.

picy Pork, Prawn, and Chicken Salad *Yum Sam Gler*

Serves 6

Sam Gler means three good friends: pork, prawn, and chicken, whose meats : combined to create this sumptuous dish. They are poached to retain their iginal flavors before being mixed with an aromatic, refreshing dressing. *amprik Pow*, chili paste with soybean oil, is essential for its pungent and 10ky chili flavor.

1/2 pound pork tenderloin
1/2 pound chicken breast, boneless and skinless
1/2 pound prawns, shelled and deveined
1 head lettuce
2 cups finely shredded cabbage, both green and red
2 cups finely shredded carrot
1/8 cup shredded red bell pepper for garnish
2 sprigs cilantro leaves for garnish

reparation: Poach or steam the meats separately as each will require a dif-rent amount of time to cook. Slice into long thin strips; set aside. Clean and it the lettuce and line a serving platter. Arrange the cabbage and carrot over e lettuce.

Dressing
1/4 cup Chili Sauce with Soybean Oil,
 Namprik Pow (see glossary)
1/4 cup fish sauce
1 tablespoon granulated sugar
1/4 cup tamarind liquid
1/4 cup lime juice
1/2 cup chopped roasted nuts for garnish

reparation: In a pot over medium heat, add the chili sauce, fish sauce, 1gar, and tamarind liquid. Bring the mixture to a boil just enough to dissolve 1e sugar. Remove from the heat and let cool. Stir in the lime juice.

–continued–

entral

139

To serve, in a bowl, combine the sliced pork, chicken, and prawn. Toss with the dressing, a little at a time and taste. Transfer the mixture onto the serving platter over the cabbage and carrot; sprinkle with the chopped nuts. Serve the remaining dressing on the side. Or arrange all ingredients decoratively in different sections like a western-style chef salad, and serve the dressing on the side.

Garnish with the red bell pepper and cilantro before serving.

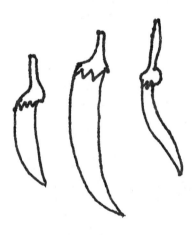

Squid Salad

Squid, or calamari, a universal ingredient, is an easy-to-find, inexpensive, delicious seafood. Quick, fresh, and clean seems to describe this recipe appropriately. Fresh squid makes it unusual and yields a satisfying, refreshing flavor and texture. The dish needs a hint of sharpness, supplied by the lime and fish sauce dressing, to tenderize the meat and cut the fishy taste.

> 1 pound squid
> 1/4 cup finely shredded young ginger
> 1 cup thinly sliced red onion
> 1 cup Chinese celery, cut into 1-inch-long pieces
> 1/4 cup mint leaves
> 1 tablespoon minced bird's-eye chilies,
>   more or less to taste
> 1 tablespoon very finely minced garlic
> 3 tablespoons fish sauce, more to taste
> 1/4 cup lime juice, more to taste
> 1 tablespoon granulated sugar (optional)
> 1/4 cup shredded red bell pepper for garnish
> 2 sprigs cilantro leaves for garnish
> 1 head lettuce

Preparation: Clean the squid and slash its surfaces into a grid pattern; cut into bite-size pieces.

In a pot, bring 3 cups water to a boil and poach the squid until done, 2 to 3 minutes. To avoid a tough and rubbery texture, do not overcook the squid. Drain and set aside.

In a bowl, combine and toss gently the rest of the ingredients *except* the red bell pepper, cilantro, and the lettuce. Transfer to a serving platter with a bed of lettuce and garnish with bell pepper and cilantro before serving.

Steamed Stuffed Eggplants
Ma-Kheua Yao Yud Sai

Serves 6

Steaming is perhaps an uncommon way to prepare this vegetable. But this dish offers an exceptional paring of eggplant's unique, soft texture and flavor combined with a sweet and sour filling. It is all around unusual in texture, flavor, and appearance.

6 whole Chinese or Japanese long eggplants
1/4 cup vegetable oil
3 tablespoons thinly sliced shallot for garnish
1/2 cup sweet basil leaves, *bai horapha*, fried for garnish
2 tablespoons minced garlic
2 tablespoons minced shallot
2 tablespoons minced cilantro root or stem
3/4 cup ground lean pork
3/4 cup chopped shrimp meat
2 teaspoons red chili sauce, *namprik dong* (optional)
2 tablespoons fish sauce
2 tablespoons soy sauce
2 tablespoons granulated sugar
1/8 cup tamarind liquid or rice vinegar
1/8 cup diced red bell pepper for garnish

Preparation: In a steamer, steam the whole eggplants for 10 to 15 minutes until soft and skin is wrinkled. Remove from the heat and let cool. Peel off and discard the skin. Cut a slit onto each eggplant to create a deep pocket without cutting all the way through. Set aside for stuffing or keep it warm in the steamer.

In a saucepan over medium heat, add the oil and separately fry the shallot and basil, until light brown and crispy. Remove and set aside for garnish.

With the same pan, add the minced garlic, shallot, and cilantro root; cook until fragrant. Add the pork and shrimp; break into small chunks. Add the red chili sauce, fish sauce, soy sauce, sugar, and tamarind liquid. Continue cooking until the pork and shrimp are done. Add some water if the texture is too dry.

To serve, spoon the stuffing into the pockets of the eggplant, mound high. Garnish with the diced bell pepper, fried shallot, and basil.

Stir-Fried Beef with Basil

Holy basil, *bai kaprow*, gives this dish authenticity and a snappy, spicy aftertaste. Holy basil is hard to find in the United States except in midsummer, when it arrives. Other basils can be substituted, but first try the authentic version. There is a holy difference. Instead of beef, pork, chicken, or seafood can be substituted.

1/4 cup vegetable oil
1 bunch holy basil, *bai kaprow*, leaves only
2 tablespoons thinly sliced shallot for garnish
3 tablespoons minced garlic
3 tablespoons minced shallot
2 cups thinly sliced beef tenderloin (1 1/2 to 2 pounds)
1/2 cup julienned carrot
1/2 cup sliced long beans or string beans, 1-inch long
1/2 cup julienned red bell pepper
1/2 cup julienned sweet Anaheim pepper
2 tablespoons minced bird's-eye chilies or red jalapeño,
    more or less to taste
2 tablespoons fish sauce
2 tablespoons oyster sauce
2 tablespoons granulated sugar
1 tablespoon rice vinegar
1 tablespoon beef or chicken bouillon

Preparation: In a wok or deep skillet over medium heat, heat the oil and fry half (1/2) of the basil leaves until crispy but not burned. Set aside for garnish. With the same oil, fry the sliced shallot until light brown and fragrant. Set aside for garnish.

In the same wok or skillet with high heat, cook the minced garlic and shallot until fragrant. Add the beef and stir-fry until almost done.

Add the carrot, long beans, bell peppers, sweet pepper, and bird's-eye chilies; stir-fry to mix well, 3 to 5 minutes.

Add the fish sauce, oyster sauce, sugar, rice vinegar, and beef bouillon; continue stir-rying until the vegetables are done to taste. Add little water if the texture is too dry.

Before removing from the heat, add the remaining unfried basil leaves and mix well. Garnish with the fried basil leaves and shallot before serving.

Stir-Fried Vegetables with Red Curry *Pad Phak Ruam Mitr*

Serves 6

This simple dish is a medley of fresh vegetables with a little twist of spicy curry. It is a break from the meat curry dishes that dominate Thai cuisine. To make it a truly vegetarian dish, substitute light soy sauce for the fish sauce and make curry paste without the shrimp paste.

3 tablespoons vegetable oil
2 tablespoons sliced shallot for garnish
2 to 3 tablespoons Red Curry Paste (page 38)
1 cup julienned carrot
1 cup sliced long beans or green beans, 1 inch long
1 cup julienned colored bell peppers
1 cup julienned baby corn
1 cup julienne bamboo shoots
2 tablespoons fish sauce or light soy sauce
2 tablespoons granulated sugar
1 tablespoon vegetable bouillon
1/2 cup basil leaves, *bai horapha* for garnish

Preparation: Heat the oil in a wok or skillet; add the shallot and fry until light brown and crispy. Remove and set aside for garnish.

In the same wok or skillet, add the curry paste and cook until fragrant. Stir in the vegetables and cook until tender.

Add the fish sauce, sugar, and vegetable bouillon; stir to mix well. If the texture is too dry, add some water.

Garnish with the fried shallot and basil leaves before serving.

Stir-fried Wide Noodles

Pad Se-Iew

Serves 4

If *Pad Thai* is the number one noodle dish, *Pad Se-Iew* is the runner-up. Wide rice noodles are used for this stir-fry dish. Sweet, dark soy sauce, *se-iew*, is the main seasoning and is essential to its flavor and color. Chicken, pork, or seafood are acceptable substitutes for beef.

Marinade:
1/2 pound beef sirloin
1 tablespoon light soy sauce
1 tablespoon oyster sauce
1 tablespoon granulated sugar
1/2 teaspoon salt
1 teaspoon ground white pepper

Preparation: Sliced the beef across the grain into thin, bite-size strips. Combine with the rest of the ingredients and marinate for at least 1 hour.

1 pound fresh wide rice noodles, *sen yai*
    (or 8 ounces dried noodles)
2 cups sliced Chinese broccoli, *gai lan*,
    or broccoli florets
1/4 cup vegetable oil
2 tablespoons sweet dark soy sauce,
    se-iew (see glossary)
2 tablespoons minced garlic
1 tablespoon light soy sauce
1 tablespoon fish sauce
1 tablespoon granulated sugar
2 whole eggs, beaten
1/2 teaspoon ground pepper

Preparation: Separate the fresh noodles into individual strands. If using dried noodles, cook in boiling water until soft and pliable. Rinse with cold water and drain.

Peel tough skins off the broccoli stems and slice into thin, bite-size pieces. Separate the stems from the leaves. Wash and set to drain.

–continued–

Central

145

In a wok or skillet over medium heat, add 2 tablespoons of the oil and swirl to coat the wok's surface. Stir in the noodles and sweet soy sauce. Cook and stir until all noodles are evenly coated; remove and set aside.

In a same wok or skillet with high heat, add the remaining 2 tablespoons oil and cook the garlic until fragrant. Stir in the marinated beef and cook until the beef is almost done for 3 minutes. Add the broccoli stems first and stir-fry for 2 minutes. Add the broccoli leaves, light soy sauce, fish sauce, and sugar; stir-fry to mix well.

Create a well in the bottom of the wok, add little oil if too dry, and scramble the eggs until firm. Stir in the noodles and mix well. Continue cooking until heated through.

Transfer to serving plates and sprinkle with the ground pepper. Serve the noodles with chili in vinegar, *Nam Som Prik Dong* (page 31), sugar, fish sauce, and chili flakes on the side.

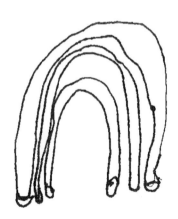

Tapioca Balls

This pork appetizer was once a common item sold by street vendors almost everywhere. A simple, but time-consuming preparation method has turned the appetizer into one of mass production, the only way to compensate for the high cost of labor. Nowadays, it can often be seen at the entrance to Thai restaurants, where the art of preparing the dish is on display to entice customers into the establishment. Chicken can be used as an alternative to pork.

Dough
1 1/2 cups small pearl tapioca
1 1/2 cups hot water

Preparation: Rinse the tapioca in cold water, drain, and transfer to a bowl. Add the hot water to the bowl a little at a time, and stir well until the texture is soft and gluey. Set aside for at least 30 minutes.

Stuffing
1/4 cup vegetable oil
1/4 cup minced garlic
1/2 cup minced onion
1 tablespoon minced cilantro
1 cup ground or minced lean pork
1/4 cup chopped roasted peanuts
1/4 cup finely chopped preserved turnip
1/4 teaspoon ground white pepper
3 tablespoons fish sauce
3 tablespoons granulated sugar
1 bunch cilantro for accompaniment
6 whole bird's-eye chilies for accompaniment
1 bunch lettuce for accompaniment

Preparation: In a saucepan over medium heat, add 2 tablespoons of the oil and fry 2 tablespoons of the garlic until light brown and crispy. Set aside both the garlic and oil for later use.

–continued–

In the same saucepan, add the remaining 2 tablespoons of the oil and cook the remaining 2 tablespoons garlic, the onion, and cilantro until fragrant. Add the pork and break it down into small chunks.

Add the peanuts, turnips, pepper, fish sauce, and sugar. Continue cooking until the pork is cooked through and liquid has been absorbed. Set aside to cool.

Roll the tapioca mixture into 1/2-inch diameter balls. Then flatten the balls into thin, 2-inch rounds. Put 1 teaspoon of stuffing in the center of each piece of the dough, pull the edges of the dough together, and seal completely. Continue making the balls until all of the dough and stuffing have been used.

Place a steamer over high heat and arrange the tapioca balls over a well-greased steam tray, using cheesecloth as liner, if necessary. Coat the balls with oil to prevent them from sticking to each other.

Steam for 15 minutes until the tapioca balls turn translucent. Remove the balls from the steamer and sprinkle with the fried garlic. Serve the tapioca balls with cilantro, chilies, and lettuce as accompaniments.

The Best of Regional Thai Cuisine

Yellow Curry Chicken

Gaeng Kari Gai

Serves 6

This mild curry has a direct Indian influence, not only the coriander and cumin but also the yellow curry powder. It is very rich and creamy, as both coconut milk and cream are used. It often requires *Ajad*, cucumber salad as an accompaniment to help clear the palate after a few bites.

2 cups peeled and diced potatoes, 1/2-inch cubes
3 tablespoons vegetable oil
3 tablespoons very thinly sliced shallot, for garnish
3 to 4 tablespoons Yellow Curry Paste (page 42)
2 cups diced chicken meat, bite-size
  (or whole drumsticks)
2 cups coconut milk
2 teaspoons salt, more to taste
2 tablespoons granulated sugar
1 cup coconut cream

Preparation: Cook potatoes in boiling water until done, 5 to 7 minutes. Do not overcook otherwise they will fall apart. Drain and rinse with cold water; set aside.

In a pot over medium heat, add the oil and fry the shallot until light brown and crispy. Remove and set aside for garnish.

In the same pot, add the curry paste and cook until fragrant. Add the chicken and stir until well coated. Add the coconut milk, salt, and sugar; cook until the chicken is done.

Add the cooked potatoes and coconut cream; heat through. Pour into a serving bowl and garnish with the fried shallot. Serve the curry with the Cucumber Salad, *Ajad* (page 98) as an accompaniment.

THE ULTIMATE
PAD THAI

When Thai cuisine is the subject of conversation in food or social circles, Pad Thai is often the place where it all starts and ends. Each chef has a signature version of this quintessential Thai dish, differing in ingredients, techniques, and leading flavors. In the Bay Area, every Thai restaurant has Pad Thai on the menu and it's usually the number one selling dish. In Thailand, you'll find street vendors and restaurants offering Pad Thai on every corner, something akin to the American burger stand. Why is this dish so popular? Maybe it's the three distinct flavors of sweet, sour, and salty mingling within each bite. Maybe it's the zesty hint of spiciness capped with a crunchy texture and nutty taste from roasted peanuts. Maybe it's the comfort food nature of noodles. The popularity of Pad Thai today will undoubtedly drive chefs and diners alike to continue their search for the Ultimate Pad Thai.

Pad Thai dates back to seventeenth century Thailand when Siam, began trading with China. The Chinese arrived with noodles, woks, and the new technique of stir-frying. Chinese chefs became employed in the Thai court, adding more variety to the royal kitchen. Chinese immigrants established an ethnic community and soon one of their noodle dishes became popular among Thai people. The dish was called "Pad Chinese" or Chinese stir-fry noodles. It consisted of medium-sized rice noodles, soy sauce, garlic chives, bean sprouts, preserved turnips, dried shrimp, sugar, and distilled vinegar. Using local ingredients and to appeal to their palate, the Thai people modified the dish by substituting the soy sauce with fish sauce, the sugar with palm sugar, and the vinegar with tamarind liquid and lime juice. They added a shrimp fat and chili powder or chili flakes for flavor and color. Other ingredients mostly remained the same. They named their dish "Pad Thai" to avoid confusion with the Chinese version. Another important difference between them was the way they were served. Pad Thai was served in a large plate with fork and spoon, accompanied by fresh vegetables such as bean sprouts, banana flowers, and green onions, while Pad Chinese was served in a bowl with chopsticks and no side vegetables.

Cooking Pad Thai is a quick and satisfying act. As a stir-fry dish, the Pad Thai takes few minutes in actual cooking. But the preparation of ingredients is the real task and must be done beforehand, making this a great dish for the social chef who likes to prepare ahead of the guest's arrival. Because we use dried rice noodles, they have to be soaked in water until pliable. Chopping and mincing the ingredients such as garlic, preserved turnips, and roasted peanuts is another key to creating the ultimate Pad Thai.

Cooking Pad Thai needs constant adjustment because heat and moisture contribute to the consistency of the noodles and the combination of flavors.

Too much moisture and not enough heat or overcooking will make the dish mushy. Not enough moisture and too much heat will make it tough and dry. If it's your first time cooking Pad Thai be patient and enjoy your research. Your ultimate Pad Thai may be many tries away, don't worry. Thai chefs make hundreds of attempts to perfect this dish.

Thai chefs in the Bay Area have experimented with ingredients from both Chinese and Thai recipes for the right combinations for their signature dish. Even when ingredients are the same, cooking techniques, ingredient preparation, and plating methods will vary. If you love Thai food and are in search of your ultimate Pad Thai start with some of the local restaurants I visited on my recent search.

At **Khan Toke** Restaurant, established twenty-five years ago on Geary Street, in San Francisco, I took off my shoes and was invited in for a Thai style dinner, sitting on the floor. Areewon, the chef, told me "we're only open for dinner and we sell more than fifty orders of Pad Thai each night." As the dining room began to fill she went on to explain, "We cook to order the Pad Thai, with either shrimp, chicken or vegetarian." I tasted her delicious dish while I concentrated on listening. She told me it was an old recipe, but had been modified. Areewon used both distilled vinegar and tamarind liquid in her recipe. Chili flakes are evident in her dish for snippy and spicy zest and visual appeal. Her parting tip was "Always observe the noodle texture while cooking, adjust the amount of liquid and heat accordingly."

Manora on Folsom, south of Market is jammed at lunch. Joe Srisopa smiles as he tells me "I sell 50 to 60 plates of Pad Thai a day, we never have enough." Joe spoke proudly "I always make sure that all flavors are combined well and seep into the grain of the noodle." A couple of orders of Pad Thai passed by my table as Joe explained "I mix all seasonings in a big batch ready to be used by our cooks so our Pad Thai always tastes the same." Joe explained his cooking process for convenience and consistency. Joe uses American ketchup in his dish mostly for the color, "I think the ketchup also gives diners a familiar taste of sweet and sour."

I climbed the steps to **Cha-Am** on Shattuck in Berkeley where the place felt more like a house than a restaurant. The manager Kay began, "We sell Pad Thai to almost every table, probably about fifty orders a day." Cha-Am also cooks Pad Thai to order accommodating any special request. Kay who has worked in other Thai restaurants observed, "The taste of Pad Thai follows the trends of customers and varies geographically." She further explained, "The chef must have experimented to find the right combination of taste for the majority of her customers … We in the restaurant business, are here to serve and will accommodate the diner the best way we can," she exclaimed.

Wat Monkhol, Thai Temple on Martin Luther King at Russell in Berkeley offers varieties of affordable Thai food every Sunday when hundreds of people line up during lunch hours. At the temple, Pad Thai is prepared only one way—vegetarian style. Yupin, the Pad Thai expert and volunteer at the temple, always cooks the dish in a big batch to accommodate a large number of people. One Sunday I assisted her in making the dish and as we prepared the gigantic wok, she told me "I always make enough to feed sixty people in three or four batches." Sometimes, she needs two assistants to help stir and lift the wok. Yupin tells me "We never know when the Pad Thai will run out, I have to be ready to make another batch. I premix all the seasonings in batches of 5 to 10 gallons at a time, and sometimes it only lasts us for a couple Sundays." To accommodate the vegetarian style, she uses salt instead of fish sauce and plenty of tofu for her dish. She exclaimed, "My vegetarian version is as flavorful, colorful, and refreshing as any meat version in the Bay Area."

7 ounces dried rice noodles, *Chantaboon*
3 tablespoons vegetable oil
2 tablespoons minced garlic
1 cup fresh shrimp, peeled and deveined
1/8 cup dried shrimp (optional)
1/4 cup fish sauce, more to taste
1/4 cup granulated sugar, more to taste
1/8 cup tamarind liquid
1/8 cup distilled vinegar, more to taste
1 tablespoon paprika or chili powder or chili flakes
2 cups sliced fried tofu
3 tablespoons very finely minced preserved turnip
2 whole eggs, beaten
1/2 cup chopped garlic chives, 1-inch long
1/2 cup chopped roasted peanuts
3 cups bean sprouts, plus more for garnish
1/2 cup shredded red bell pepper or chili for garnish
5 sprigs cilantro leaves for garnish
1 whole lime, cut in wedges for garnish

reparation: Soak the rice noodles in warm water until pliable about 30 min-
tes. Change the water several times as necessary. Drain and set aside.

Ieat a wok over high heat, add the oil, and cook the garlic until fragrant. Add
oth shrimp and cook until done. Add the noodles and stir until well coated
rith oil.

dd the fish sauce, sugar, tamarind liquid, vinegar, and paprika (these ingredi-
nts can be combined ahead of time). Stir-fry the mixture until thoroughly
ombined and the liquid is absorbed. Check the noodle texture, it should be
ooked and soft. Add some water if needed. Stir in the tofu and turnip.

reate a well at the center of the wok, add the eggs and scramble until firm.
dd the chives, peanuts, and bean sprouts; stir-fry to mix well.

ransfer to a serving plate, then garnish with the red pepper and cilantro.
erve with extra fresh bean sprouts and lime wedges.

Pad Thai Salad

6 ounces cellophane noodles or
glass noodles, *woon sen*
1/2 cup dried mouse's-ear mushrooms
(or 1 cup other fresh mushrooms)
2 cups prawns, peeled and deveined
1/2 cup vegetable oil
3 tablespoons thinly sliced shallot for garnish
3 tablespoons thinly sliced garlic for garnish
1/2 cup dried shrimp for garnish
1 cup julienned colored bell peppers
1 cup thinly sliced celery
1 cup bean sprouts
1/4 cup garlic chives or scallion, cut 1 inch long
1 bunch romaine lettuce, shredded to bite-size
1/2 cup roasted half peanuts for garnish
5 sprigs cilantro leaves for garnish

Preparation: Cook the noodles in boiling water until soft and clear. Strain and plunge into cold water to stop cooking. Drain and cut into a manageable length; set aside to dry. Soak the dried mouse's-ear mushrooms in warm water until soft and fully expanded. Slice into thin, long strips.

In a pot, bring water to a boil and poach the prawns until done, about 3 minutes. Strain and cut in half lengthwise; set aside. Poach the mushroom until done about 3 minutes. Strain and set aside.

In a pan over medium heat, heat the oil and fry the shallot until light brown and crispy. Remove and drain over absorbent papers. Fry the garlic and dried shrimp the same way; set aside for garnishes.

Dressing
1/4 cup fish sauce
1/4 cup granulated or palm sugar
1/8 cup tamarind liquid
1/8 cup distilled vinegar
2 tablespoons minced preserved turnips
1 tablespoon paprika or chili powder
1/8 cup lime juice
1 tablespoon minced red bird's-eye chili,
    more or less to taste

Preparation: In a pot over medium heat, combine the fish sauce, sugar, tamarind liquid, vinegar, preserved turnips, and paprika. Bring the mixture to a boil and cook until it turns syrupy. Remove from the heat and let cool. Stir in the lime juice and chili.

To serve, combine the noodles, prawns, mushrooms, bell pepper, celery, bean sprouts, and garlic chives in a large mixing bowl. Toss with the dressing, a little at a time, and adjust the taste according to your preference.

Transfer to a serving platter with a bed of lettuce. Sprinkle with the fried shallot, garlic, dried shrimp, peanuts, and cilantro leaves.

South
Roi Dee

Tropical Beaches and Rain

Cashew nuts, *Mamoung Himmaphan*, which grow abundantly in the South, are a major part of a local legend and an ingredient in the delicious dish, Chicken with Cashew Nuts (page 164). The cashew nut is a seed that develops outside the fruit of the mango. Cashew is sought after for its unique flavor and texture, and can be eaten by itself as a snack or as an ingredient in many dishes. It is quite expensive even where it is grown.

There once was a forest called Himmaphan, about which many legends and stories have been told in Thai literature. A one-of-a-kind tree stood in this forest, and, over time it developed an enormous, stable trunk whose branches extended over a vast area. For many years, the tree produced only one very precious fruit, which guarded and protected like a mother.

Above the forest stood a mountain of immeasurable mass and height, on which gods and angels resided. One day, one of the chief angels fell ill and no cure could be found from within the vast mountain. So the angels were sent off to collect herbs and spices from the Himmaphan forest to be used in different potions for a cure, but alas, to no avail.

As the chief angel's condition worsened to near death, he dreamed of the precious fruit from the old tree. The angels were once again dispatched urgently, this time to seek this fruit as the cure. The lone fruit was plucked from the tree and successfully cured the chief angel. However, this left the mother tree severely weakened and saddened by her loss. With little life remaining, the tree managed to produce one more fruit as the only seed for the next generation, but she could not wait for the fruit to ripen and fall to the ground. As she struggled to try to separate the seed from the fruit so that the seed could have a chance to live rather than die with her, the fully recovered chief angel, on his way to the tree to show her his gratitude, witnessed this peculiar activity. He ordered the tree to freeze, with the words *"Yar Roung,"* "don't drop"; hence, the seed was left dangling peculiarly on the bottom and outside of the fruit. And so, *Yar Roung* is the name Southerners gave the tree, which came to reproduce the *Mamoung Himmaphan*, mango of the Himmaphan forest, throughout the Southern region.

The Southern peninsula stretches down between the Gulf of Thailand and the Indian Ocean. The long shorelines carry the wealth from the sea to most Southern cities. Beautiful beaches attract tourists from around the world and big investments in resort and hospitality businesses. Phuket Island, for example, has earned the reputation of being a first-class tourist destination, with its tropical paradise, convenient international airport, and luxury hotels.

Many Southern beaches have been featured in numerous movies, notably "The Beach" and "Diamonds Are Forever." The landscape of the South varies dramatically from rolling green rice fields in the Central region to the tall trees of rubber plantations. Other common terrains include the sloping hills with coconut palm and spiky pineapples. These plantations are watered by a nearly eight-month rainy season. Some parts of the South still have dense jungles, which have been preserved for rare and endangered animal species.

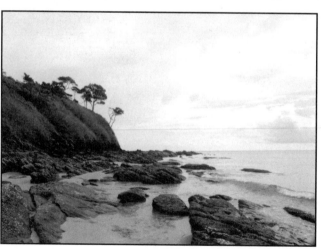

The South experiences and accepts greater religious diversity than the other regions. A concentration of Muslims in the South constitutes the second largest religion in the Thai kingdom. The Southern language is the most distinctive and difficult to comprehend according to the Central standard. Farther south near the Malaysia border, the Southerners also speak Malay and have absorbed a Malay way of life. Southern cuisine reflects the neighboring influence of Malaysia, with Muslim curries and avoidance of pork. Coconut is locally produced and presented in many regional dishes. Seafood dishes, *Pla Phao*, grilled fish, or *Goong Seap*, prawn skewers, are ingeniously prepared in a unique Southern way. *Gaeng Leung*, yellow soup, and *Kaeng Tai Pla*, fish tripe soup, owe their origins to the South, where their special ingredients grow. An indigenous plant, *Sataw*, is produced only in this region and transported all over Thailand as a Southern delicacy.

Ever popular, the South receives tremendous amounts of tourists, who bring in wealth to local people, especially in well-known destinations such as Phuket and Samui Island. Standard of living among these places had increased so drastically that some places are financially beyond the reach for most Thai

people. The Southern food scene caters to Western visitors. Local food has been modified to accommodate the Western palate. I've often found the taste too far in between to be anything good. Fortunately in most restaurants, the local dishes still maintain the taste and integrity of Thai cuisine.

Barbecued Whole Fish (Phuket)

Pla Phao Phuke

Serves

Phuket is a beautiful island and tourist destination of the South. Twenty years ago I had my first Phuket barbecued fish, and I still recall how fresh and sweet the meat was. The fish, a colorful parrotfish, was caught and grilled right on the white sandy beach. A local friend used coconut husk for fuel, which enhanced it with a smoky aroma. By the time the sun dipped into the ocean, our fish dinner was ready. Eating the fish unadorned was exhilarating, and eating it with the sauce was divine.

1 whole fresh fish, 2 to 2 1/2 pounds

Preparation: Select a fresh saltwater fish such as parrotfish, red and white snapper, black pomfret, sea bass, or halibut. Clean and gut the fish but leave the head, skin, and scales attached.

Prepare a firewood or charcoal grill ahead of time so it reaches medium heat. Place the whole fish on the grill and cook, turning occasionally until done, at least 15 minutes on each side. Make sure that the heat is even under the fish.

After the fish is done, peel off and discard the skin. The meat should be tender and juicy but not dry. Serve the fish with the dipping sauce.

Dipping Sauce
1/4 cup palm sugar
1/4 cup fish sauce
3/4 cup tamarind liquid
1/2 cup very thinly sliced shallot
10 whole bird's-eye chilies, chopped,
   more or less to taste

Preparation: In a bowl, dilute the palm sugar with 2 tablespoons warm water. Add the rest of ingredients and stir to mix well. Serve the sauce on the side.

Braised Chicken Curry

The South produces plenty of coconuts and exports its large surplus. The remainder goes into many regional dishes, especially in curries. Malaysia has had an influence on this dish and made it one of the most popular dishes of the deep South. American fried chicken is a perfect and readily available substitute for the dish.

> 1 whole spring chicken or an equal
>   amount of fried chicken
> 2 tablespoons butter
> 2 tablespoons vegetable oil
> 3 tablespoons Red Curry Paste (page 38)
> 1 tablespoon curry powder
> 1 tablespoon turmeric
> 4 cups coconut milk
> 1/4 cup fish sauce
> 3 tablespoons lime juice
> 3 tablespoons palm sugar
> 2 tablespoons shredded red bell pepper for garnish
> 2 sprigs sweet basil leaves, *bai horapha*, for garnish

Preparation: Cut the chicken into 8 to 10 pieces. In a pan or skillet over medium heat, combine the butter and oil. Fry the fresh chicken until well brown. Remove the chicken and set aside. Or use already-fried chicken.

In the same pan, combine the curry paste, curry powder, and turmeric; cook until fragrant.

Add the fried chicken and coconut milk to the pan. Stir to mix well and bring to a boil. Reduce the heat to low and simmer for 20 minutes.

Stir in the fish sauce, lime juice, and palm sugar. Continue cooking until the sugar is dissolved. Sprinkle with the garnishes and serve.

Chicken with Cashew Nuts *Gai Pad Med Mamuang Himmaphan*

Serves 6

Cashew nuts are an essential commodity of the South where they grow commercially. They are a superb ingredient in many dishes for their unique flavor and texture. This dish calls for chicken to complement the crunchy and nutty cashews. The combination has made the chicken with cashew nuts one of the best Thai stir-fry dishes.

3 tablespoons vegetable oil
6 whole dried bird's-eye chilies
2 tablespoons chopped garlic
2 cups sliced chicken breast, cut into bite-size pieces
1 cup sliced onion
1 cup julienned colored bell peppers
1 tablespoon fish sauce
1 tablespoon sweet dark soy sauce
1 tablespoon oyster sauce
1 tablespoon granulated sugar
1 tablespoon chicken bouillon
1 cup roasted cashew nuts
1/4 cup green onion, cut 1 inch long, for garnish
3 sprigs cilantro for garnish

Preparation: In a wok over high heat, add the oil and fry the dried chilies until crispy. Remove from the oil and set aside.

Add the garlic to the wok and cook until fragrant. Stir in the chicken and cook for 3 minutes. Add the onion and bell pepper; stir-fry to almost done for 3 minutes.

Add the fish sauce, soy sauce, oyster sauce, sugar, and chicken bouillon. Stir to mix well and cook until the chicken and vegetables are done. Add the cashew nuts and fried chilies. Continue cooking until heated through.

Transfer the mixture to a serving platter and garnish with the green onion and cilantro before serving.

Panaeng Beef Curry

Malaysia has had a strong influence on Thai cuisine, such as this dish, which originally came from the city of Penang on the southern boarder of Thailand. Beef is usually the choice of meat for religious reasons, as Malaysia and southern Thailand are predominantly Muslim. In the Central region, the dish has been adapted locally using all kinds of meat, such as pork and prawns. Whatever meat is used, it should be cooked until tender and the sauce fully absorbed. Shredded kaffir lime, both in the curry paste and garnish, is needed to tie all flavors together.

> 2 tablespoons vegetable oil
> 3 tablespoons Panaeng Curry Paste (page 37)
> 2 cups diced beef tenderloin, 1/2-inch cubes
> 2 cups coconut milk
> 1/4 cup fish sauce
> 3 tablespoons palm sugar
> 4 tablespoons shredded kaffir lime leaves
> 1/4 cup julienned onion
> 1 cup julienned red bell pepper
> 2 tablespoons finely chopped roasted nuts
> 2 sprigs sweet basil leaf, *bai horapha*, for garnish

Preparation: In a pot over medium heat, add the oil and cook the panaeng curry until fragrant. Add the beef and stir until well coated.

Add the coconut milk, fish sauce, and palm sugar; bring the mixture to a boil. Reduce the heat to simmer and continue cooking until the beef is tender, about 10 minutes. The mixture should be somewhat thick.

Stack 4 kaffir lime leaves and roll tightly into a cigarette-like roll. Slice the roll thinly and unravel into thin, long strips.

Add the onion, bell pepper, and roasted nuts; simmer for 5 minutes until the vegetables are done. Garnish with the shredded kaffir lime and basil leaf before serving.

Rice Salad

Healthful and delicious, this dish is filled with vegetables, fiber and minerals, and recent research shows that lemongrass, galangal, and kaffir lime have medicinal properties. Yet the dish has no fat, and hardly any cooking is required. It can easily be a Southern chef salad with local ingredients and snappy, tasty dressing.

2 cups steamed rice
1 cups shredded coconut or coconut flakes
1 cup dried shrimp
1 cup peeled and seeded pomelo or
  grapefruit segments
1/2 cup shredded green mango or
  Granny Smith apple
1/2 cup shredded star fruit
1/2 cup sliced long beans, round and very thin
1/2 cup sliced cucumber, small and thin
2 stalks lemongrass, tender part
5 whole kaffir lime leaves
1 cup bean sprouts

Preparation: Roast the coconut in dry pan over a stove or in a 350°F oven until light brown and fragrant, about 5 to 7 minutes.

In a mortar with pestle or food processor, process the dried shrimp until ground.

Peel of the outer shell of the lemongrass and cut off the hard root. Slice the tender part cross-section into very thin rings. Stack the kaffir lime leaves and roll into a tight cigarette-like roll. Slice across the roll very thinly and unravel into long, thin strips.

Arrange all ingredients side by side on a big serving platter. Serve with the dressing on the side.

The Best of Regional Thai Cuisine

Dressing (Nam Boodoo)
2 tablespoons chopped lemongrass
2 tablespoons chopped galangal
2 tablespoons chopped garlic
1/4 cup chopped shallot
3 whole kaffir lime leaves
1/4 cup shrimp paste or anchovy
2 tablespoons fish sauce
1/2 cup palm sugar

Preparation: In a pot over medium-low heat, combine all ingredients with 2 cups water and cook until thick—almost to a syrup consistency, about 15 to 20 minutes. Strain the mixture through a fine sieve.

To serve, spoon salad ingredients in an individual serving plate and sprinkle with the dressing. Toss to mix well before eating.

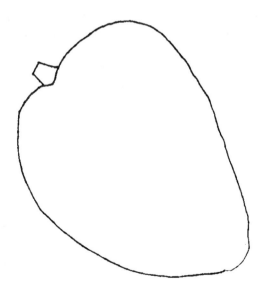

Scallop Salad

In the United States, scallops from the cold sea are much larger, meatier, and more tender than Thai scallops. They are superb for this refreshing, delicate salad. Do not overcook scallops or they will turn rubbery. For best results, undercook them a little bit to retain their sweetness, and let lime juice cure them to perfection.

> 1 pound scallops, shelled
> 1 cup sliced Chinese celery,
>   both stems and leaves, cut 1 inch long
> 1 cup thinly sliced red or yellow onion
> 1 cup sliced tomato, seeded
> 2 tablespoons minced bird's-eye chilies,
>   more or less to taste
> 1/4 cup fish sauce, more to taste
> 1/4 cup lime juice, more to taste
> 2 teaspoons granulated sugar (optional)
> 1 head lettuce for accompaniment
> 2 tablespoons chopped green onion for garnish
> 3 sprigs cilantro leaves for garnish

Preparation: Poach the scallops in boiling water for 2 to 4 minutes; drain and cut into thin slices. Do not overcook otherwise they will be tough and rubbery.

In a bowl, combine the scallops with the rest of ingredient *except* the lettuce and garnishes, and toss to mix well. Adjust the taste with more fish sauce and lime juice.

Transfer the mixture to a serving platter with a bed of lettuce. Garnish with the green onion and cilantro before serving.

Shrimp Fat Fried Rice

Khao Pad Mun Goong

Serves 4

Shrimp fat is bright orange and extracted from the chief of shrimp or prawns. It is also available prepackaged in a jar. It has a rich, creamy shrimp-based flavor and, cooked in rice, its fragrance permeates and dominates this one-of-a-kind fried rice. A squeeze of lime brightens up the entire dish.

> 3 tablespoons vegetable oil
> 2 tablespoons finely minced garlic
> 1 tablespoon minced shallot
> 1 tablespoon finely minced cilantro root or stem
> 1/2 teaspoon ground black pepper
> 2 tablespoons shrimp fat
> 1 cup shrimp, peeled and deveined
> 2 tablespoons light soy sauce
> 1 tablespoon Maggi seasoning
> 2 cups steamed rice (leftover old rice preferred)
> 1 tablespoon granulated sugar
> 2 tablespoons chopped cilantro leaves for garnish
> 1 whole lime, wedged, for accompaniment
> 1/2 cup sliced cucumber for accompaniment
> 1/2 cup sliced tomato for accompaniment
> 6 stalks green onion for accompaniment

Preparation: In a wok or skillet over medium heat, add the oil and cook the garlic, shallot, cilantro root, and ground pepper until fragrant. Add the shrimp fat and shrimp; cook until fragrant and the shrimp are done. Add the light soy sauce and Maggi seasoning; stir to mix well.

Fluff the rice to fully separate and add to the wok. Sprinkle with the sugar and continue cooking and stirring until all ingredients are heated through.

Transfer to serving plates and top with the cilantro. Serve the fried rice with the accompaniments.

Three Flavor Prawn

Goong Sam Ros

Serves 6

Large prawns or lobsters are abundant in the South both wild and commercially raised, and are easily affordable. This dish allows the fresh prawn flavor to really shine, with a complementary and delicate salty, sweet, and sour sauce. It may become all seafood lovers' favorite.

6 whole large prawns (3 per pound, U-3)
1 cup vegetable oil
1 cup sweet basil leaves, *bai horapha*, for garnish
2 tablespoons chopped garlic, for garnish
2 tablespoons sliced shallot, for garnish
10 whole dried small red chilies, for garnish
2 tablespoons fish sauce
1/4 cup palm sugar
1/4 cup tamarind liquid
1 tablespoon shrimp or chicken bouillon
1/4 cup chopped roasted cashew nuts

Preparation: Cut the prawns open, butterfly style, from head to tail leaving the shells attached. Clean and rinse with cold water; set aside to dry.

In a pan over medium heat, add the oil and separately fry the sweet basil leaves, garlic, shallot, and dried chilies until light brown and crispy. Remove and drain over absorbent papers for garnishes.

In the same pan, fry the prawns until done, 2 to 3 minutes on each side. Transfer to a serving platter, lined with the fried sweet basil.

In the same pan with little oil, add the fish sauce, sugar, tamarind liquid, and shrimp bouillon. Continue cooking until the sugar is dissolved and the sauce turns syrupy, about 7 to 10 minutes. Add water as necessary.

To serve, pour the sauce over the fried prawns. Sprinkle with the crispy shallot, garlic, chilies, and cashew nuts for garnish.

ellow Rice Buried Chicken   *Khao Buree or Mok Gai*

Traveling through Southeast Asia I've seen this dish in Indonesia, Malaysia, Myanmar, Singapore, and Thailand. Each has subtle differences according to local taste, but the main influence must have been from Persia and India, as a similar dish shows up in those cuisines.

1 whole chicken (2 pounds)
2 cups long-grain rice, jasmine or basmati rice
4 whole cardamom seeds
2 whole nutmegs
3 whole cloves
3 sticks cinnamon
2 cups milk
1 cup chicken stock
1/4 cup sour cream
1 tablespoon ground turmeric
1/2 cup chopped onion
1/4 cup golden raisins
1 teaspoon salt
1 tablespoon chicken bouillon
3 tablespoons vegetable oil
2 tablespoons thinly sliced shallot for garnish
2 tablespoons butter, melted
1 piece cheesecloth

Preparation: Skin the chicken and cut into body parts: breasts, thighs, drumsticks, and wings; set aside. Rinse the rice with cold water and set aside to drain.

Smash the cardamom seeds and wrap in cheesecloth along with the nutmegs, cloves, and cinnamon sticks. Secure the cheesecloth tightly.

In an ovenproof pot with lid over medium heat, combine the milk, chicken stock, and sour cream. Add the wrapped spices and turmeric; bring the mixture to a boil.

Stir in the rice, onion, raisins, salt, chicken bouillon, and chicken. Continue cooking, lid covered, over low-medium heat for 20 minutes.

–continued–

In a small-size pan, heat the oil and fry the shallot until light brown and crispy Remove and drain over absorbent papers. Preheat the oven to 350°F.

Pour the butter over the rice and sprinkle with the fried shallot. Transfer the pot with lid onto the preheated oven and cook for another 15 minutes until the rice and chicken fully done. Serve the rice with Chili Sauce and Cucumber Salad, *Ajad* (page 98).

Chili Sauce

5 whole chopped fresh red chilies,
   prik chee fa, serrano, or jalapeño
1 tablespoon chopped garlic
1 tablespoon chopped cilantro root or stem
1 teaspoon ground cumin
1 tablespoon chopped mint leaves
1/4 cup lime juice
1 tablespoon granulated sugar
1 teaspoon salt

Preparation: In a mortar with pestle or food processor, process the chilies, garlic, cilantro root, cumin, and mint leaves until they form a smooth paste. Add the lime juice, sugar, and salt; stir until the sugar is dissolved. Serve the sauce on the side with the rice.

Yellow soup with pickled bamboo shoots from the South is known to be very hot and pungent. But the taste is so satisfying with its subtle sourness of pickled bamboo and the essence of fresh turmeric. It is easy to see that the South uses a lot of turmeric in its cuisine.

> 2 pounds pickled bamboo shoots
> 3 tablespoons Southern Yellow Curry Paste (page 40)
> 1 pound fish fillet, cut into 2-inch cubes
> 1/4 cup fish sauce, more to taste
> 1/4 cup tamarind liquid
> 2 tablespoons palm sugar
> 2 tablespoons lime juice, more to taste

Preparation: Rinse the bamboo shoots several times with water to get rid of the strong flavor or poach in boiling water. Cut the bamboo shoots into bite-size pieces.

In a pot, bring 4 cups water to a boil and stir in the chili paste. Add the bamboo shoot and cook over medium heat for 10 minutes.

Add the fish, fish sauce, tamarind liquid, and sugar. Bring the mixture to a boil and continue cooking until the fish is done.

Remove the pot from the heat and stir in the lime juice. Adjust the taste with more fish sauce and lime juice before serving.

Desserts and Beverages

Thai savory dishes are highlighted internationally, but unfortunately, its desserts fall below par. Most Thai desserts hardly suit the Western palate because of their rich coconut, plain sweetness, and primarily heavy texture. But Thai fruits make up for the lack of popularity of the desserts in their quality, variety, and exciting flavors.

In Thailand, most desserts are also served as snacks and light meals that can be eaten at any time. Sweet rice with mango and fried bananas, for example, are served at all hours and are not necessarily eaten at the end of the meal.

Somehow, among the many kinds of desserts, not more than a handful make it to U.S. and international markets. These dishes, the pioneers of Thai dessert, are being adapted to suit the Western palate, and hopefully, in the not too distant future, all Thai desserts will gain their much-deserved spotlight.

Banana Pudding in Coconut

10 to 15 Thai bananas,
   kluai nam wa or *kluai khai*
3 cups coconut milk
1 cup palm sugar
1 teaspoon salt
1 teaspoon pandan or vanilla extract (optional)
1/2 cup coconut cream

Preparation: Peel the bananas and cut into quarters.

In a pot over medium heat, add the coconut milk and bring it to a boil. Add the bananas and cook until the bananas are tender for 5 minutes.

Add the sugar, salt, and pandan extract, if using. Stir gently until the sugar is dissolved.

Remove from the heat and stir in the coconut cream. Serve the pudding while still warm.

Banana Puree Cake

Kanom Kluai

Serves 6

3 ripe bananas, *kluai hom*
3 ripe Thai bananas, *kluai nam wa*
5 ripe baby bananas, *kluai kai*
3 tablespoons rice flour
1 tablespoon cornstarch
1 teaspoons salt
1 cup shredded fresh coconut or
   coconut flakes
2 cups coconut cream
1/2 cup granulated sugar
1/2 cup palm sugar

Preparation: In a food processor, peel and combine all bananas. Add the rice flour and cornstarch; process until they form a paste. Set aside. Combine the salt and shredded coconut; set aside.

In a bowl, combine the coconut cream, granulated sugar, and palm sugar; stir until the sugars are dissolved. Add the banana mixture and stir to mix well.

Transfer the final puree to an 8-inch square aluminum or glass baking tray suitable for a steamer. Spread mixture to level. Sprinkle with 3/4 of the shredded coconut and steam in a steamer with high heat for 15 to 20 minutes. Or bake in a 375°F oven over a water tray for 15 to 20 minutes.

Remove from the heat and set cool. Cut the banana puree into bite-size pieces. Sprinkle with the remaining shredded coconut and serve with ice cream.

Instead of steaming in the baking tray, small containers made of banana leaves would also be very attractive presentation.

Coconut Custard

1 cup coconut cream
1 cup finely chopped or melted palm sugar
6 whole eggs
1/2 teaspoon jasmine or vanilla extract
1/8 teaspoon salt

Preparation: Combine all ingredients in a bowl and beat with a fork for 2 minutes. Do not overbeat to prevent air bubbles from forming. Strain the mixture through a fine sieve.

Pour the mixture into an 8-inch square baking dish and steam over high heat for 15 to 20 minutes. Or bake in a 375°F oven over a water tray for 15 to 20 minutes or until a knife inserted into the custard comes out clean.

Let cool and cut into bite-size pieces for serving. The custard can also be served with Sweet Sticky Rice (page 192).

Instead of steaming in the baking tray, small containers made of banana leaves would make a very attractive presentation.

Coconut Custard in Cones   *Kanom Krow Sunkaya*

Serves 4 (30 Pieces)

Stuffing
1 bunch banana leaves
1 teaspoon jasmine, pandan, or vanilla extract
1/2 cup palm sugar
1/2 cup granulated sugar
1 cup rice flour

Preparation: Cut the banana leaves into 7-inch-diameter circles. Cut the circles in half and roll them into cone shapes and hold them in shape with toothpicks. On the top layer of the steamer, stand the cones up by inserting their pointy tips in the steamer holds.

To make jasmine water, add the jasmine extract to 1 1/4 cups water. In a medium-size pot, combine both sugars with the jasmine water and bring to a boil. Stir until the sugars are dissolved. Remove from the heat and let cool.

Put the flour in a bowl and slowly add half of the sugar mixture and knead until soft. Then add the rest of the sugar mixture and mix well.

Pour the stuffing into cones 3/4 way up. Place the top steamer over boiling water, cover with a lid, and cook for 5 minutes.

Topping
2 whole large eggs
1/2 cup palm sugar
1 cup coconut cream

Preparation: Combine all ingredients and strain through a fine sieve.

Pour the topping over the cooked stuffing to almost fill the cones. Continue steaming for another 5 minutes until the topping is firm up. Let cool and serve.

Coconut Ice Cream

Ice Cream Kati

Serves 6

1 ripe coconut or 3 1/2 cups coconut milk
1 cup granulated sugar

Preparation: For best results, freshly squeezed coconut milk is desirable for a refreshing sweet flavor. Open a ripe coconut and shred the white meat into fine flakes or extract the white meat from the shell and process in the food processor until it forms a paste.

In a medium-size bowl, add the shredded coconut and pour in 1 cup of hot water. Steep the coconut for 5 minutes. Knead and squeeze the milk through a fine sieve. Repeat the process until obtaining 3 1/2 cups coconut milk.

In a small-size pot over medium heat, combine the sugar and 1/2 cup water. Cook until the mixture is reduced to a thick syrup consistency, and coats a spoon, about 5 to 7 minutes. Remove from the heat and let cool to lukewarm. Add the coconut milk and stir to mix well.

Pour the mixture into an ice cream maker and process for 45 minutes until stiff. Coconut ice cream must be kept cold because it melts rapidly.

For extra flavors and textures, add chopped fruit such as jackfruit and mango to the coconut mixture before freezing.

Crunchy Water Chestnuts "Pomegranate" *Tubtim Krop*

Serves 4

1 1/2 cups fresh water chestnuts
Red food coloring
1/2 cup cornstarch
1 cup granulated sugar
1 cup coconut cream
1 teaspoon jasmine, rose, or vanilla extract
2 cups crushed ice

Preparation: Peel and dice the water chestnuts into 1/8-inch squares. Sprinkle with the food coloring, creating light and dark red spots to imitate the look of pomegranate seeds. Fold in the cornstarch to coat evenly, shaking off the excess starch.

In a small-size pot, bring 3 cups water to a boil. Add the water chestnuts and cook until they are floating on the surface. Cook the water chestnuts a little bit at a time and gently stir so they do not stick to each other. Strain them from the hot water and immediately plunge in very cold water. Remove from the cold water and set aside.

To make the syrup, boil the sugar with 2 tablespoons water. Cook until the sugar is dissolved and thick. Remove from the heat and then add the coconut cream and jasmine extract. Stir to mix well and set aside to cool.

To serve, combine the water chestnuts with coconut syrup. Portion into serving bowls and top with the crushed ice.

Floating Sweet Tapioca

1 cup small pearl tapioca
1/4 cup hot water
1/4 cup dried lotus seeds
1 1/2 cups coconut milk
1/2 cup palm sugar
1/2 cup granulated sugar
1/2 cup coconut cream

Preparation: Place the tapioca in a bowl and slowly add the hot water. Mix and knead the mixture until smooth and tender.

Cook the dried lotus seeds with boiling water until tender enough to be mashed between your fingers, and drain. In a food processor, process the lotus seeds into a fine paste and set aside.

Roll the tapioca into 1/4-inch-diameter balls. Flatten the balls into thin rounds and stuff with the lotus paste. Seal the lotus paste completely with the tapioca dough.

Cook the stuffed tapiocas in boiling water until they are floating to the surface. Remove them from the hot water and plunge into cold water to prevent them from sticking to each other. Remove and drain.

In a pot over medium heat, combine the coconut milk and sugars; stir until the sugars are dissolved. Bring the mixture to a boil and add the cooked tapioca.

Bring the mixture to a boil once more and remove from the heat. Stir in the coconut cream and serve.

Fried Bananas

1 3/4 cups coconut milk
1/2 cups granulated or palm sugar
One 12-ounce package banana batter mix,
  or 1 1/2 cups (from Thai grocery stores)
  OR instead of batter mix, combine
    1/2 cup rice flour
    1/2 cup all-purpose flour
    1/4 cup potato flour
    1/4 cup cornstarch
    1 tablespoon baking powder
1/2 teaspoon salt
1 cup grated fresh coconut or coconut flakes
1/4 cup sesame seeds (optional)
3 cups vegetable oil for deep-frying
10 whole Thai bananas, *kluai nam wa*, or plantain
  (sweet potato and taro can also be used)

Preparation: In a medium bowl, beat the coconut milk and sugar gently until the sugar is completely dissolved. Add the batter mix. Whisk the mixture with a wire beater until smooth and then fold in the salt, grated coconut, and sesame seeds.

In a pan over medium heat, heat the oil to 350° to 375°F for deep-frying. Peel and cut the bananas into thin, bite-size pieces. Dip the bananas in the batter to coat completely and carefully lower into the hot oil. Fry and turn the bananas until golden brown on all sides, 10 to 15 minutes.

Serve the fried bananas with ice cream or fruit sorbet.

Fried Bananas with Eggs

Kluai Tod

Serves 6

2/3 cup coconut cream
2 whole eggs
1/4 cup palm sugar
1/2 cup rice flour
1/2 cup all-purpose flour
1 tablespoon baking powder
1/4 teaspoon salt
3 cups vegetable oil for deep-frying
10 whole Thai bananas, *kluai nam wa* or plantain
  (sweet potato and taro can also be used)

Preparation: In a medium bowl, beat the coconut cream, eggs, and palm sugar gently until the sugar is completely dissolved. Add the mixture of flours, baking powder, and salt. Whisk the mixture with a wire beater until smooth. Cover and refrigerate for at least 30 minutes.

In a pan over medium heat, heat the oil to 350° to 375°F for deep-frying. Peel and cut the bananas into thin, bite-size pieces. Dip the bananas in the batter to coat completely and carefully lower into the hot oil. Fry and turn the bananas for 10 to 15 minutes or until golden brown on all sides.

Serve the fried bananas with ice cream or fruit sorbet.

Mung Bean Cake

3/4 cup dried mung beans
3 tablespoons vegetable oil
1/4 cup thinly sliced shallot
6 whole eggs
2 cups coconut cream
1 1/2 cups palm sugar
1 teaspoon jasmine or vanilla extract

Preparation: Soak the mung beans in plenty of cold water overnight or at least 3 hours. Drain before cooking.

In a pot over medium heat, simmer the mung beans with 3 cups water until soft, enough that they can be mashed between your fingers. Add more water if needed. Remove from the heat and drain; let cool.

In a pan over medium heat, add the oil and fry the shallot until light brown and crispy. Set aside.

In a blender or food processor, add the mung beans and process until smooth. Add the eggs, coconut cream, sugar, and jasmine extract. Process for 2 minutes until the sugar is dissolved and all ingredients are well combined.

Preheat the oven to 350°F. Pour the mixture into 8 x 8-inch baking pan and bake for 15 minutes. Sprinkle the fried shallot all over the surface of the cake and continue baking for an additional 10 minutes or until a knife inserted at the center of the cake comes out clean.

The cake can be served hot or cold, with vanilla or coconut ice cream.

Palm Nut Cake

1 cup ripe palm fruit meat,
   luk tan or ripe apricot
3 cups rice flour
1 1/2 teaspoons baking powder
1 1/2 cups coconut cream
2 cups granulated sugar
1 bunch banana leaves or small ramekins
1 cup shredded fresh coconut or coconut flakes
1/8 teaspoon salt

Preparation: In a bowl, combine the palm meat, rice flour, sugar, and baking powder. Slowly add the coconut cream, a little at a time, and mix and knead until the mixture is well combined. Cover the bowl with a thin cloth and leave to set for 2 to 3 hours.

Cut the banana leaves into 3-inch diameter circles. With small toothpicks or staplers, fold and hold the edges to make small round containers. Instead of the banana leaves, small ramekin can be used.

Fill the containers with the palm mixture to almost full. Steam the cakes in a steamer over high heat for 20 minutes until a knife inserted in the center of the cake comes out clean.

Combine the shredded coconut with the salt and set aside for garnish.

To serve, take the cakes out of the containers and fold the cake with the shredded coconut. Or serve the cakes in the banana containers with the shredded coconut sprinkled on top.

Pandan Sweet Gelatin *Woon Bai Toey*### Bottom Layer
1 bunch pandan leaves or
  4 1/2 teaspoons pandan extract
2 tablespoons plain unflavored gelatin powder
1 1/4 cups granulated sugar
12 small molds (any shape, usually flowers or animals)
12 orchid flowers or rose petals for decoration

Preparation: Boil 8 cups of water with the shredded and bruised pandan leaves. Cook until the water turns green and fragrant about 10 minutes. Strain and discard the solid. Measure out 4 1/2 cups pandan water. Reserve the rest. Or dilute pandan extract with 4 1/2 cups water to make pandan water.

Combine the gelatin with pandan water and bring to a boil. Add the sugar and stir to dissolve. Pour the gelatin mixture into the molds 3/4 way up, then refrigerate until set and firm, about 20 minutes.

Top Layer
2 tablespoons unflavored gelatin powder
1 3/4 cups pandan water (or 1 3/4 teaspoon pandan
  extract with 1 3/4 cups water)
1 cup granulated sugar
3 cups coconut cream
1/2 tablespoon rice flour
1/2 teaspoon salt

Preparation: Combine the gelatin with pandan water and bring to a boil. Add the sugar and stir to dissolve. Combine the coconut cream, flour, and salt. Add the mixture to the boiling gelatin. Simmer and stir for 5 minutes until well mixed.

Pour the mixture over the bottom layers in the molds and set to cool in the refrigerator until set and firm, about 20 minutes. Unmold and serve the gelatin upside down with flower decoration. The finished gelatin should have dark green color at the top and light green at the bottom. Reverse the colors by reversing the process.

To be more creative, add any diced fresh fruit to the bottom layer for more interesting flavor and texture.

Desserts and Beverages

Pumpkin Custard

1 whole medium-size pumpkin or
  Japanese kobocha (2 pounds)
1 cup palm sugar
3 whole pandan leaves, cut 2 inches long and
  bruised (or 1 teaspoon pandan extract)
1 cup coconut cream
1 tablespoon cornstarch
1/8 teaspoon salt
6 whole eggs, beaten

Preparation: Carve an opening on top of the pumpkin and save the top for lid. Use a sturdy spoon to clean out seeds in the pumpkin cavity. Set aside to use as a container.

In a small-size pot over medium heat, melt the sugar with the pandan leaves. Stir in the coconut cream, cornstarch, and salt; cook and stir until the sugar completely dissolves. Do not let it boil. Discard the pandan leaves.

Add the eggs and stir constantly with a whisk. Continue stirring and making sure that the mixture is not forming lumps or not burning at the bottom. Cook and stir until the mixture has a texture of smooth thick gravy.

Pour the mixture into the pumpkin and transfer to a steamer. A wok with a tight lid can also be used as a steamer. Steam the pumpkin with its top on the side over high heat for 30 to 45 minutes until done (when a knife inserted at the center of the custard comes out clean and the texture is firm). Let cool.

To serve, warm or cold, slice the pumpkin into wedges and serve. It can also be served with vanilla or coconut ice cream.

Pumpkin Pudding in Coconut   *Fakthong Gaeng Buat*

Serves 6

2 pounds pumpkin
4 cups coconut milk
3/4 cup palm sugar
1/4 cup granulated sugar
1/2 teaspoon salt
1 cup coconut cream

Preparation: Peel the pumpkin and remove the seeds and white membranes from the cavity. Slice the meat into 1/2-inch-thick and 2-inch-long strips.

In a pot over high heat, combine the coconut milk, 1 cup water, palm sugar, granulated sugar, and salt. Bring the mixture to a boil and stir until the sugars are dissolved.

Add the pumpkin and cook until tender about 7 to 10 minutes. Do not overcook otherwise the pumpkin will fall apart.

Stir in the coconut cream and bring the mixture to just a boil once again. Remove from the heat and serve while still warm.

Sesame Seed Balls

2 1/2 cups all-purpose flour
1/2 teaspoon baking powder
1/2 teaspoon baking soda
1/4 teaspoon salt
3/4 cup granulated sugar
2 large eggs
2 tablespoons butter, melted
1/2 cup white sesame seeds
3 cups vegetable oil

Preparation: In a small-size bowl, combine the flour, baking powder, baking soda, and salt; mix thoroughly.

In a pot over medium heat, combine 1/4 cup water with sugar and cook until the sugar is dissolved and turns syrupy. Set aside to cool.

In a medium-size bowl, beat the eggs until soft peaks form. Slowly add butter, a little at a time, and beat to mix well.

Add the flour mixture and syrup into the egg mixture. Mix and knead until soft and smooth. Portion the mixture into golf-ball-size balls. Roll the balls over the white sesame seeds until thoroughly coated.

In a pan over medium heat, heat the oil to 350° to 375°F and fry the balls until golden brown, stirring to turn frequently. Remove from the oil and drain over absorbent papers. Serve the balls with hot tea.

Shredded Coconut Cake

Kanom Babin
Serves 4

1 ripe coconut or 2 1/2 cups grated coconut
2 1/2 cups glutinous rice flour
6 Asian jasmine flowers or
   1 teaspoon jasmine or vanilla extract
1 large egg
2 cups granulated sugar

Preparation: Cut the fresh ripe coconut in half and discard the juice. Shred the white coconut meat with a hand grater or extract the white meat from the shell and shred in a food processor. Measure out 2 1/2 cups.

To make jasmine water, float the full bloom jasmine flowers in 1 cup of water overnight or dilute the jasmine extract with 1 cup of water.

Combine the rice flour, shredded coconut, and jasmine water. Knead the mixture until all liquid is absorbed. Add the egg and continue kneading until well mixed.

Transfer the mixture to a medium pot over medium heat. Add the sugar and stir until the sugar is dissolved and the mixture thickens.

Preheat the oven to broil. Pour the mixture into a greased 6 x 6-inch baking pan and spread to level the surface. Put the pan near the heat source and cook until the surface turns golden brown. Let cool and cut to serve.

Or form the mixture into 1/4 inch thick and 3-inch diameter patties. In a flat-bottom pan over medium heat, with a little oil, fry the patties until golden brown on both sides.

The coconut cake can also be served with vanilla or coconut ice cream.

Sticky Rice and Mangoes *Khao Neaw Mamoung*

2 cups sweet, sticky, or glutinous long-grain rice
1 cup palm sugar
3 pieces pandan leaves, cut 2 inches long,
    bruised or 1 teaspoon pandan extract
3 cups coconut cream
3/4 teaspoon salt
3 whole ripe mangoes
2 tablespoons roasted black sesame seeds or
    mung beans for garnish

Preparation: Soak the rice in cold water overnight or at least 2 hours. In a steamer over high heat, drain the rice and steam over cheesecloth if necessary. Stir and turn the rice occasionally. Sprinkling the rice with cold water while steaming helps reduce cooking time. Steam the rice until tender, for 20 to 30 minutes.

In a pot over medium heat, melt the sugar with the pandan leaves. Stir in the coconut cream and salt. Cook until the sugar is dissolved. Discard the leaves.

When the rice is ready, transfer to a bowl. While the rice is still hot, stir in 3/4 of the coconut mixture and combine thoroughly.

To serve, peel the mangoes and slice into bite-size pieces. Arrange the mango and sticky rice on a serving plate and top with the remaining coconut mixture. Sprinkle with the roasted sesame seeds or mung beans before serving.

ticky Rice Stuffed Banana   *Khao Tum Mud*

2 cups sweet, sticky, or glutinous long-grain rice
1 cup black beans
4 cups coconut cream
1 1/4 cups palm sugar
1/8 teaspoon salt
1 bunch banana leaves for wrapping
10 ripe Thai bananas, *kluai nam wa*
1 cup shredded coconut for garnish
1/2 cup granulated sugar for garnish

reparation: Soak the sticky rice and black beans separately in cold water vernight, or at least 2 hours. Drain the rice and beans before cooking.

1 a pot over medium heat, combine
1e rice, coconut cream, palm sugar,
nd salt. Cook the rice mixture and stir
ccasionally until the liquid is absorbed.
1ake sure that the rice is not burned at
1e bottom and the texture is glue-like.
1 another pot over medium heat, cook
1e beans with 4 cups water until ten-
er. Drain and set aside.

ut the banana leaves into 7 x 8-inch rectangular pieces. Use two pieces of aves with their grains running in opposite directions to make a wrapper. Peel 1e bananas and cut in half lengthwise.

pread the rice mixture thinly at the center of the wrapper, the size a little big-er than the sliced banana. Place a piece of banana at the center of the rice and p with more rice to cover banana completely. Sprinkle with black beans. Vrap the contents tightly with the wrappers and tuck the edges underneath. ontinue wrapping until all rice and bananas have been used.

rrange the wrapped bananas in a steamer and cook over high heat for 30 1inutes until the rice is fully cooked.

erve the stuffed banana as it is, or unwrap and slice it into bite-size pieces. prinkle with the shredded coconut and sugar.

Tapioca with Tropical Fruits

3/4 cup small pearl tapioca
2 cups sliced assorted tropical fruits
both fresh and preserved, save 1 cup of syrup
(mango, lychee, longan, rambutan, palm seed,
pineapple, etc.)
1 1/2 cups granulated sugar
2 cups coconut cream
1/8 teaspoon salt
1 teaspoon jasmine or vanilla extract
1 bunch orchids for garnish

Preparation: Rinse the tapioca with cold water.

In a pot, bring 4 cups water to a boil and add the tapioca pearls; stir constantly
Reduce the heat and simmer for 10 to 15 minutes until all the pearls are soft
and clear. Stir in 1 cup reserved fruit syrup.

Add 1 cup of sugar, 1 cup of coconut cream, salt, and jasmine extract. Stir to
combine and cook until the sugar is fully dissolved. Remove from the heat
and stir in the sliced fruits, reserving some fruit for garnish.

Combine the remaining 1 cup coconut cream and 1/2 cup sugar to make a
topping.

Pour the pudding in serving bowls, top with the topping and garnish with the
reserved sliced fruits and orchids. Serve warm or cold.

Taro Coconut Cake

Kanom Maw Gaeng Pheuak

Serves 4

1 1/2 cups peeled and diced taro
5 whole eggs, slightly beaten
1/2 teaspoon salt
1 1/4 cups coconut cream
1 tablespoon all-purpose flour
1 1/4 cups palm sugar
3 tablespoons vegetable oil
2 tablespoons very thinly sliced shallot

Preparation: Cook the taro in boiling water until tender so that they can be mashed between your fingers. Remove and drain. In a blender or food processor, combine the cooked taro, eggs, and salt; process until smooth.

In a bowl, combine the coconut cream, flour, and sugar. Stir or beat until the sugar is dissolved. Add the taro mixture to the bowl and stir to mix well.

In a pan over medium heat, add the oil and fry the sliced shallot until light brown and fragrant. Set aside over absorbent papers.

Preheat the oven to 350°F, pour the mixture in an 8 x 8-inch baking pan and bake for 20 to 30 minutes or until the surface is golden brown. Remove from the oven and garnish with the fried shallot.

Slice the cake into small portions and serve warm or cold.

Taro and Coconut Pudding

Pheuak Gaeng Buat

Serves 4

2 cups coconut milk
1 cup peeled and diced taro, 1/2-inch cubes
1 cup palm sugar
1/2 cup coconut cream

Preparation: In a pot over medium heat, bring the coconut milk to a boil then add the diced taro. Cook until half way done, about 5 minutes.

Add the sugar and continue cooking until the taro is done about 5 minutes. Before removing from the heat, add the coconut cream and then serve.

Thai Cupcakes

Kanom Tuay

Serves 4 (30 pieces)

Bottom Layer
12 Asian jasmine flowers or
  2 1/2 teaspoons jasmine or vanilla extract
3/4 cup rice flour
2 1/2 cups palm sugar

Preparation: To make jasmine water, float 12 fully blooming jasmine flowers in 1/2 cups of water overnight or dilute jasmine extract with 2 1/2 cups of water.

In a bowl, combine all ingredients stir until the sugar is dissolved.

In a steamer with water at a full boil, heat 30 small ramekins. Pour the mixture into the ramekins 3/4 way up and cook until firm, about 7 minutes.

Top Layer
1/4 cup rice flour
2 cups coconut cream
1 teaspoon salt

Preparation: In a bowl, combine all ingredients and gently beat until smooth.

Pour the mixture on top of the cooked bottom layers to almost fill the ramekins. Continue cooking in the steamer until the top layers are firm, another 7 minutes.

To serve, run a small blade around the ramekins to loosen the mixture. Turn the ramekins over on a serving platter and remove the ramekins to expose the cupcakes.

Mung Bean Drink

2 pounds mung beans or yellow beans
1/2 cup margarine
2 tablespoons brown cane sugar
1/8 teaspoon salt

Preparation: Rinse the beans with cold water and set aside to dry.

In a thick skillet over medium heat, dry roast the beans until light brown. Add the rest of the ingredients and stir to mix well, remove from the heat and let cool.

Process the beans in a grinder and brew the same way you do with coffee beans. Serve with sugar and cream the same way you serve a cup of coffee.

Thai Iced Coffee

Cafae Yen

Serves 4

1 cup ground coffee, your choice
1/2 cup granulated sugar (optional)
3/4 cup condensed milk
3/4 cup half-and-half or milk
3 cups crushed ice

Preparation: Brew the coffee with 4 cups boiling water to make very strong coffee. Add the sugar and stir until dissolved. Set aside to cool in a refrigerator.

Combine the condensed milk with half-and-half and stir to mix well.

To serve, fill a tall glass with ice and pour in the cold coffee 3/4 way up. Top with the condensed milk mixture before serving.

Thai Iced Tea

Thai tea is a blend of tea leaves, herbs, and spices under the name Thai Seasoning Mix or Cha Thai. It is available in a 1-pound package in well-stocked Asian grocery stores.

> 1/2 to 3/4 cup Thai tea (seasoning mix)
> 3/4 cup granulated sugar, more or less to taste
> 3/4 cup sweetened condensed milk
> 1 pint cream, half-and-half, or milk
> 3 cups crushed ice

Preparation: Bring 8 cups water to a boil, add the tea, and brew for 10 minutes. Strain the tea through a fine sieve and discard the solids. Add the sugar and stir until dissolved. Set aside to cool in a refrigerator.

Combine the condensed milk and the cream, stirring to mix well.

To serve, fill a tall serving glass with the crushed ice. Pour the tea up to 3/4 of the glass and top with the condensed milk mixture; stir well.

RESOURCES

Chompituk, Yuvadee. *Arhan Thai See Phak*. Bangkok: Rungsang Printing, 1998.

Culinaria Konemann. *South Asian Specialties*. Cologne: Konemann, 1998.

Gruenwald, Joerg. *PDR for Herbal Medicines*. Montcale: Medical Economic Company Inc., 1998.

Heymann-Sukpan, Wanphen. *The Foods of Thailand*. New York: U.S. Media Holdings Inc., 1996.

Kongpun, Sisamon. *The Best of Thai Dishes*. Bangkok: Sangdad Books, 2000.

Mahidol University. *The Miracle of Veggies 108*. Bangkok: Kopfai Publishing, 1997.

McNair, James. *Cooks Southeast Asia*. San Francisco: Chronicle Books, 1996.

Owen Sri. *Classic Asian*. London: DK Publishing Inc., 1998.

Poladitmontri, Panurat. *The Thai Beautiful Cookbook*. San Francisco: CollinsPublishers, 1992.

Sawedvimon, Sunti. *Tumnan Arhan Thai*. Bangkok: Nanmeebooks, 1999.

Thanakit. *50 Nitan Thai*. Bangkok: Sureewiyasarn Printing, 1996.

Thonanong, Thongyao. *Royal Court Recipes*. Bangkok: Sangdad Books, 1998.

Von Holzen, Heinz. *The Food of Indonesia*. Singapore: Periplus Editions (HK) Ltd., 1999.

Walden, Hilary. *The Encyclopedia of Creative Cuisine*. London: Quarto Publishing Limited, 1986.

Yu, Su-Mei. *Cracking the Coconut*. New York: Harper Collins Publishers Inc., 2000.

RECIPE INDEX

APPETIZERS & SALADS

MAIN COURSES

ONE-PLATE DISHES

DESSERTS and BEVERAGES

INDEX

Also available from Hippocrene...

Dictionaries/Language Studies

THAI-ENGLISH/ENGLISH-THAI DICTIONARY & PHRASEBOOK
JAMES HIGBIE
Thai belongs to the Tai language family, a group of related languages spoken in Thailand and Laos and by minority ethnic groups in Burma, northern Vietnam and southern China. This book provides a basic grammar, and the vocabulary and phrases a traveler might want to know. All Thai words are spelled in the English alphabet only, thus making it an easy reference for people unfamiliar with Thai script.
2,500 entries ▪ 197 pages ▪ 3 3/4 x 7 1/2 ▪ 0-7818-0774-3 ▪ $12.95pb ▪ (330)

LAO-ENGLISH/ENGLISH-LAO DICTIONARY & PHRASEBOOK
JAMES HIGBIE
Designed for travelers and people living in Laos and northeastern Thailand, this dictionary and phrasebook features the phrases and vocabulary of modern, spoken Lao. The two-way dictionary contains over 2,500 entries; the 49-section phrasebook provides practical cultural information and the means for communication in daily life and travel-related situations. Each Lao word is romanized, and pronunciation is indicated as well. The Lao language, also called Isan, has over 15 million speakers.
2,500 entries ▪ 206 pages ▪ 3 3/4 x 7 1/2 ▪ 0-7818-0858-8 ▪ $12.95pb ▪ (179)

LAO BASIC COURSE
WARREN G. YATES AND SOUKSOMBOUN SAYASITHSENA
This course is designed to give students a general proficiency in conversational Lao. Short lessons introduce students to basic grammar and vocabulary while exercises reinforce newly-introduced concepts. Each section contains helpful notes on special difficulties in the language.
423 pages ▪ 5 1/2 x 8 1/2 ▪ 0-7818-0410-8 ▪ $19.95pb ▪ (470)

Cookbooks

THE BEST OF TAIWANESE CUISINE
KAREN HULENE BARTELL

Dishes from the four corners of China are found in Taiwanese kitchens and restaurants: noodles, dumplings and Mongolian Lamb Barbecue from northern China; sauces and herbs from the east featured in recipes like "Piquant Lime Chicken in Swallow's Nest;" the hot, spicy, fried foods from the Szechuan region; and foods from southern China such as lightly seasoned, fresh seafood. More than a collection of over 100 delicious Taiwanese recipes, this cookbook is divided into seasons and traditional celebrations such as Lunar New Year, Dragon Boat Festival, Chinese Valentine's Day, and Mid-Autumn Moon Festival—with a complete menu for each one. Complementary and harmonious foods are organized in 18 carefully planned menus.
122 pages ▪ black & white photos/drawings ▪ 0-7818-0855-3 ▪ $24.95hc ▪ (46)

JAPANESE HOME COOKING
HANS KIZAWA AND RINA GOTO-NANCE

Husband and wife team Hans and Rina have put together this unique collection of recipes for "comfort foods" and meals eaten every day in typical Japanese households. With its emphasis on fresh seafood and vegetables, Japanese cuisine is very healthful and is gaining popularity throughout North America. Among these 100 recipes are all varieties of sushi and miso soups, along with other specialties like "Sukiyaki," "Cold Somen with Ham and Veggies," "Tofu Steak with Mushroom," and "Squid and Daikon." Photographs illustrating techniques and sections on equipment, basic ingredients, and Japanese pronunciation ensure that even novice cooks can produce spectacular results. Full of little anecdotes and observations, this book will be a delightful addition to any North American kitchen.
160 pages ▪ 5 1/2 x 8 1/2 ▪ $24.95hc ▪ 0-7818-0881-2 ▪ (27)

HEALTHY SOUTH INDIAN COOKING
ALAMELU VAIRAVAN AND PATRICIA MARQUARDT

With an emphasis on the famed Chettinad cooking tradition of southern India, these 197 mostly vegetarian recipes will allow home cooks to create fabulous exotic fare like Masala Dosa with Coconut Chutney, Pearl Onion and Tomato Sambhar, Chickpea and Bell Pepper Poriyal, and Eggplant Masala Curry. These easy-to-prepare dishes are exceptionally delicious and nutritious, featuring wholesome vegetables and legumes flavored with delicate spices. Each of these low-fat, low-calorie recipes includes complete nutritional analysis. Also included are sample menus of complementary dishes and innovative suggestions for integrating South Indian dishes into traditional Western meals. A section on the varieties and methods of preparation for dals (a lentil dish that is a staple of the cuisine), a multilingual glossary of spices and ingredients, and 16 pages of color photographs make this book a clear and concise introduction to the healthy, delicious cooking of South India.

348 pages ▪ 5 1/2 x 8 1/2 ▪ 16 pages color photographs ▪ 0-7818-0867-7 ▪ $24.95hc ▪ (69)

THE INDIAN SPICE KITCHEN: ESSENTIAL INGREDIENTS AND OVER 200 AUTHENTIC RECIPES

MONISHA BHARADWAJ

This richly produced, wonderfully readable cookbook, written by the food consultant to the celebrated London restaurant, Bombay Brasserie, takes you on an unforgettable culinary journey along the spice routes of India with over 200 authentic recipes and stunning color photographs throughout. Simple step-by-step recipes, all adapted for the North American kitchen, allow the home chef to create delicious foods with precious saffron, aromatic tamarind, and delicately fragrant turmeric, mustard and chilies.

The recipes are arranged by featured ingredient in a full range of soups, breads, vegetarian and meat dishes, beverages, and desserts. Among those included are "Lamb with Apricots," "Cauliflower in Coconut and Pepper Sauce," and "Nine Jewels Vegetable Curry." This cookbook includes historical and cultural information on each ingredient, facts on storing and preparation, medicinal and ritual uses, and cooking times and serving suggestions for all recipes.

240 pages ▪ 8 x 10 1/4 ▪ color photographs throughout ▪ 0-7818-0801-4 ▪ $17.50pb ▪ (513)

IMPERIAL MONGOLIAN COOKING : RECIPES FROM THE KINGDOMS OF GENGHIS KHAN

MARC CRAMER

Imperial Mongolian Cooking is the first book to explore the ancient culinary traditions of Genghis Khan's empire, opening a window onto a fascinating culture and a diverse culinary tradition virtually unknown in the West.

These 120 easy-to-follow recipes encompass a range of dishes—from Appetizers, Soups and Salads to Main Courses (Poultry & Game, Lamb, Beef, Fish & Seafood), Beverages and Desserts. Among them are "Bean and Meatball Soup," "Spicy Steamed Chicken Dumplings," "Turkish Swordfish Kabobs," and "Uzbek Walnut Fritters." The recipes are taken from the four khanates (kingdoms) of the empire that include the following modern countries: Mongolia,

Chinese-controlled Inner Mongolia, China, Bhutan, Tibet, Azerbaijan, Kyrgyzstan, Tajikistan, Turkmenistan, Uzbekistan, Kazakhstan, Georgia, Armenia, Russia, Poland, Ukraine, Hungary, Burma, Vietnam, Iran, Iraq, Afghanistan, Syria and Turkey. The author's insightful introduction, a glossary of spices and ingredients, and list of sample menus will assist the home chef in creating meals fit for an emperor!
211 pages ■ 5 1/2 x 8 1/2 ■ 0-7818-0827-8 ■ $24.95hc ■ (20)